THE LAWYER'S GUIDE TO
GOVERNING YOUR FIRM

ARTHUR G. GREENE

ABA **LawPracticeManagementSection**

MARKETING • MANAGEMENT • TECHNOLOGY • FINANCE

Cover design by Jim Colao.

Nothing contained in this book is to be considered as the rendering of legal advice for specific cases, and readers are responsible for obtaining such advice from their own legal counsel. This book and any forms and agreements herein are intended for educational and informational purposes only.

The products and services mentioned in this publication are under or may be under trademark or service mark protection. Product and service names and terms are used throughout only in an editorial fashion, to the benefit of the product manufacturer or service provider, with no intention of infringement. Use of a product or service name or term in this publication should not be regarded as affecting the validity of any trademark or service mark.

The Law Practice Management Section of the American Bar Association offers an educational program for lawyers in practice. Books and other materials are published in furtherance of that program. Authors and editors of publications may express their own legal interpretations and opinions, which are not necessarily those of either the American Bar Association or the Law Practice Management Section unless adopted pursuant to the bylaws of the Association. The opinions expressed do not reflect in any way a position of the Section or the American Bar Association.

Library of Congress Cataloging-in-Publication Data
The Lawyer's Guide to Governing Your Firm. Arthur G. Greene:
Library of Congress Cataloging-in-Publication Data is on file.

10-digit: ISBN 1-59031-780-7
13-digit: ISBN 978-1-59031-780-8

12 11 10 09   5 4 3 2 1

Discounts are available for books ordered in bulk. Special consideration is given to state bars, CLE programs, and other bar-related organizations. Inquire at Book Publishing, American Bar Association, 321 N. Clark Street, Chicago, Illinois 60654.

Contents at a Glance

Contents

Chapter 6
Financial Challenges 33

Chapter 7
Revenue Opportunities 41

Chapter 8
Partner Accountability   49

Chapter 9
Partner Compensation   57

Chapter 10
Professional Legal Staff 67

Chapter 11
Practice Groups 79

Chapter 12
Succession Planning   85

PART III
A STEP-BY-STEP GUIDE TO BETTER GOVERANCE   91

Chapter 13
Strengthening the Partnership   93

About the Author

Arthur G. Greene is a law firm consultant with Boyer Greene, L.L.C., with locations in Michigan, New Hampshire and Nevada. He brings to his consulting practice over 35 years experience as a practicing lawyer, during which he served both as managing partner of a large New Hampshire firm and as the founder of a small firm. His consulting practice focuses on both practice management and the strategic and financial aspects of maintaining a healthy firm. He conducts profitability studies, facilitates retreats, and provides guidance and recommendations on a variety of management topics, including strategic planning, paralegal utilization, attorney/client dynamics, alternative billing methods, partner compensation and law firm mergers. Mr. Greene has written and lectured on most law firm management topics and is an adjunct professor at Franklin Pierce Law Center and is a Fellow of the College of Law Practice Management.

Acknowledgments

I have many friends and colleagues to thank for their help with this book. Over the years, the active members of the Law Practice Management Section of the ABA have been a source of inspiration and guidance to me. Included among those deserving particular thanks are Beverly Loder, former LPM Executive Editor, Carole Levitt, my project manager and reviewer, Denise Constantine, LPM Publishing Book Production Manager, Kimia Shelby, LPM Publishing Editorial Assistant, and to Timothy Johnson, LPM Executive Editor, whose steady hand and patience with my repeated blown deadlines are worthy of special recognition and appreciation.

I also want to thank my partner, Sandra J. Boyer, for her assistance and collaboration, particularly on issues of associate training and mentoring which is the subject matter of her latest ABA book. And, an important thank you to Kathy Williams-Fortin, a respected author in her own right, for her important advice on a number of the topics and her careful review of every aspect of the book. Her contribution has made the book substantially better than it might have been.

It's All About the Culture

Good governance and a positive culture go hand in hand. A firm's culture is the result of attitudes, personalities, policies, and decisions, past and present. The culture goes to the very heart of governance issues and is either a building block upon which good governance can propel the firm to new levels of success, or a hindrance which stands in the way of meaningful improvement. It is rare to find a law firm that has reached success without having a superior culture, in which each person is provided with the best possible environment to succeed, free of distracting internal strife and unnecessary stress.

A law firm's culture cannot be determined by a vote of the partners or established by decree of the firm leadership. It cannot be created by a mission statement or a written policy. Rather, the culture is the firm's overall fabric wherein all the intangible aspects are woven together.

Too often, we hear about law firm cultures in decline, or a struggling firm that looks successful from the outside but is perceived by those on the inside as dysfunctional. There is no doubt that current trends in the legal profession have adversely impacted most law firm cultures. Increased focus on the billable hour, the 24/7 pace, the increased associate salaries, technology, marketing/advertising, and competition from mega-firms and from non-lawyers, have taken their toll on the profession. A troubled culture that cannot be changed may result in a firm destined to muddle in failure.

Changing a culture is not easy to accomplish and success is not to be assumed. Underlying attitudes and behaviors change slowly, if at all. But, the good news is that lawyers can create a shift in their firm's culture through a unified and persistent effort. It will only happen, however, if all the lawyers are committed to the effort as a priority and act as positive role models.

Understanding the Impact

1

What Does Culture Have to Do with Governance?

People are at the heart of any law firm. For better or worse, partners have the ability to shape the firm's culture. Associates learn from the partners and, as they mature, will begin to mimic partner behaviors, all of which will send clear signals as to the range of tolerant behavior. The resulting attitudes will cause veiled limits on the nature and scope of any improvements to the firm's governance and to the possibility of the firm achieving new levels of success.

Setting the Tone

Partners can be enthusiastic and upbeat, creating a positive work environment that propels everyone to work at their highest performance level. The tone may be relaxed, but with a professional atmosphere in which every person understands what is expected and is motivated to be productive and effective in making their individual contributions to the firm's goals and objectives. On the other hand, if the partners are ineffective, pessimistic, or unhappy, the negative vibes will permeate the entire office and will lower expectations.

The Staff-Driven Culture

While the lawyers' attitudes and behaviors can have the greatest influence on firm culture, there are firms with staff-driven cultures. In most cases, staff-driven cultures are the result of a vacuum due to the lawyers' lack of interest in setting a consistent tone, or due to the absence of effective leadership.

Staff-driven cultures are rarely positive in nature and often need to be transformed.

The Heavy Hand of Times Past

Lawyers in firms with a long history must realize that their firm's culture may be a legacy left by generations of former partners. Longstanding staff members, who have survived the departure of their bosses, may have an inordinate influence on the firm's culture. A negative culture that has survived from the olden days will present a huge challenge, but the possibility of change becomes realistic once the significance of the historical influence is acknowledged.

Molding the Culture

A strong firm leader committed to change is the first step in improving the firm's culture. The leader will need a vision for the firm's future, while at the same time thinking strategically and being receptive and fair minded. An effective leader needs to have the partners' trust and confidence as well as the ability to motivate those he or she is charged with leading.

Lawyer Recruitment

If your firm is relatively new, you have an opportunity to mold the firm's culture based on the policy decisions and the hiring decisions going forward. While the same opportunity exists for firms will a long history, the challenge is greater.

Regardless of past mistakes, the activity of hiring lawyers, whether entry level or lateral, needs to focus on more than the candidates' law school transcripts and books of business. After all, it is the personalities, attitudes, and behaviors of the people that drive the culture. Because of that, there are certain personal characteristics that vigilant lawyers look for in building a partnership with a positive culture. Keep in mind the qualities that will be most important in shaping the firm's culture in the years ahead, some of which are set out below:

- **Collegiality:** Are they likely to care about and get along with you and everyone else in the firm? Are they able to manage their ego and be a team player? Are they generous in spirit? Do they have any idiosyncrasies that would drive you or others crazy?
- **Attitude:** Are they optimistic in nature? Do they have a can-do attitude? At the same time, are they realistic in their approach and their

expectations? Are they entrepreneurial and do they have a progressive attitude?

- **Shared values:** Are they honest and ethical? Will they share your concern as to the quality of the work? Will they treat staff with respect? Will they share your view as to the importance of client service? Will they exhibit an ability to put the firm's interests ahead of their personal goals?
- **Common purpose and direction:** Will they share the partners' common purpose and direction? Diversity is important, as is a variety of compatible practice areas. But, in the last analysis, the partners need to come together and focus on a common purpose and a common direction.
- **Commitment:** Will they be committed to the firm? Will they be serious in their approach to the firm and their role in its success? Are they prepared to be accountable for their contribution? While the whole area of work ethic has become an issue in many firms as generational differences cause strains to develop, there can be an accommodation of differences, as long as there is an unyielding commitment to the firm and to each other.
- **Adaptability to change:** Will they be open to change? Do they have an ability to consider other views and compromise? Will they be flexible in doing what is necessary for the sake of the firm?

Personal characteristics can be difficult to judge in a job interview setting but should not be overlooked as a significant consideration. Attention to the firm's evolving culture with each hiring decision will have a profound affect on its governance and the firm's ability to succeed.

Troublesome Behaviors and Tough Decisions

Most firms have at least one disruptive partner. The partner is often out of step with the others and creates controversy at every turn. The partner may be hard on the staff or just difficult to get along with. The partner may be a bully or self-centered, believing the staff exists primarily to serve his or her needs. Unfortunately, one person can be enough to prevent the necessary change in the firm's culture.

From a governance standpoint, the question becomes whether the disruptive partner's financial contribution is so significant that the firm needs to tolerate the behavior at the expense of impeding improved governance and all of the well behaved partners, associates, and staff.

Too often, law firms will ignore partners' personal idiosyncrasies and tolerate troublesome situations. By not addressing these problems, firm management will lose credibility in trying to deal with other issues. Action may be necessary, even if it causes short-term pain or financial challenges.

Similar issues pertain to staff members who are not exhibiting desirable behaviors and are having a negative effect on other staff members. An unwillingness to pitch in and help lawyers other than their individual boss is far too typical. In many firms, the problem staff member seems untouchable, perhaps due to the fact that the troublesome behavior has been tolerated for decades. Unfortunately, failure to make tough decisions on issues such as this will interfere with a well-meaning firm leadership's ability to achieving the firm's goals and objectives.

Whether a partner or a staff member, the problem person is undoubtedly having a negative impact on a broader group of people. Don't underestimate the effect of a "bad apple" on the firm and be sure to take appropriate action.

Ensuring a Highly Productive Staff

With properly selected people and the necessary synergy, a working group can yield results greater than the sum of its parts. Or, as is more likely in many law firms, the opposite can be true.

Successful firms have learned that good skills and the willingness to cooperate with others are critical considerations in selecting staff.

Hire the best candidates available to you. Qualifications are important. But take it one step beyond the skill set. Don't underestimate the importance of a cooperative, team-focused can-do approach. Ask yourself if the applicant is the type of person who can get along and cooperate with others. Can this person put the firm's goals ahead of individual needs? Will he or she support others as part of an integrated staff? Look for employees who appreciate what it takes to participate in a way that best contributes to the firm's success.

Your staff members are the "face" of the firm. Your staff will have the first opportunity to make an impression on new clients and potential clients. There is no amount of good lawyering that can effectively overcome a client's initial bad experience with a staff member.

Protecting the Law Firm 2

Protecting the law firm as an institution is the cardinal rule for setting up a firm towards the path of success. Although the term "institution" may sound bureaucratic, negative, and unhelpful to lawyers in a small or medium-sized firm, this couldn't be more wrong. Simply put, it means that the law firm comes first and decisions need to be made based on what is best for the firm, as opposed to what is best for any individual.

Do You Have a Law Firm or a Group of Lawyers?

Too often, smaller firms are composed of several lawyers running individual practices in what amounts to little more than an office-sharing situation. Unfortunately, this can be true of some medium-sized firms as well. In these situations, there is no firm or institution in the true sense. Instead, there are only individual practices pretending to be in a firm setting. The lawyers may practice under the same roof and have a common name on the shingle hanging by the front door, but there is no "firm" existence as the term is commonly understood.

The lawyers in these small and medium-sized firms do not appreciate the advantages they could reap from a law firm concept. They naively think that a shared roof and common shingle by the door make them a law firm. These lawyers need to take a hard look at their situation and recognize that their lack of an institutional attitude is holding them back.

A firm with an institutional focus has many of the following characteristics:

Comprehensive Partnership Agreement

A firm with an institutional approach has a comprehensive partnership agreement (or bylaws or operating agreement, depending on the entity structure). In addition to setting forth the rights and responsibilities of the partners, the agreement is designed to protect the firm from potential actions of individual partners. To protect the institution, the agreement should include:

- *Accountability standards.* What is expected of partners in terms of commitment, productivity and advancing the interests of the firm?
- *Partner admissions.* Does the partner admission process focus on the need for lawyers with similar core values and does it give attention to the type of lawyer needed to advance the interests of the firm?
- *Partner expulsions.* What behaviors are so harmful to the firm they would result in either automatic or discretionary expulsion?
- *Voluntary departures.* How does the firm protect itself from adverse impacts due to partner departures? To what extent does the firm want to include disincentives in the partnership agreement?
- *Disability.* How does the firm protect itself from the adverse effects of carrying a partner struggling with an unexpected disability?
- *Death.* What are the rights of a deceased partner and how does the firm structure its obligations to the partner's estate?
- *Valuation issues.* How is the firm to be valued? Any departures, for whatever reason, may result in a financial impact on the firm requiring that a valuation process be in place.

Leadership

The firm's leaders, by their example, will set the tone and will demonstrate the importance of advancing the firm's interests in all actions and communications with the partners and the firm as a whole. The firm will need:

- *Capable leadership.* Without capable leadership, it will be impossible to get the lawyers focused on the advantages of protecting the institution.
- *Strong centralized management.* Once firms adopt the policies necessary to promote the firm as an institution, management needs to implement those policies and make certain they are honored and respected as core ingredients for moving the firm to greater success.
- *Meaningful reporting.* The firm's management needs to be certain the lawyers receive information on all issues, but in particular fi-

nancial information that is prepared in a format that is relevant, simple to understand, and meaningful to the goals the firm seeks to achieve.

■ *An external focus.* Firms need to minimize the amount of lawyer time and energy used for debating and discussing internal firm issues at the expense of having an external focus directed at competing in the marketplace.

Compensation System

A law firm with an institutional approach will have a compensation system that rewards lawyers who best advance the firm's interests, rather than those lawyers who are focused primarily on their own individual success:

■ *Fair method of dividing the profits.* In the final analysis, the compensation must be perceived as fair.

■ *Management tool.* The compensation system should be used as a management tool to reward desired behaviors and penalize behaviors that are harmful to the firm's efforts as a whole.

■ *"Raise all the boats."* Lawyers need to understand that all partners can share in the firm's financial success when they make decisions that focus on improving the firm's revenue.

Firm Policies

The policies adopted in conjunction with the partnership agreement and culture will also reveal whether the firm is focused on protecting the institution. For example, the firm may need to establish:

■ *Associate promotion.* The firm should have criteria for partnership that includes not only consideration of both the quality of the candidate's efforts in all respects, but also whether the firm (the institution) needs or will benefit from the additional partner.

■ *Productivity requirements.* The firm needs a revenue budget and each lawyer needs to understand the extent of his or her responsibility to contribute to the revenue.

■ *Client intake standards.* When decisions must be made as to the matters that the firm should handle, intake issues should not be left to the predilections of individual lawyers.

These are some of the characteristics of a successful law firm that focuses on its success as an institution. Lawyers in firms without an institutional focus should look carefully at how the firm's structure may prevent achieving higher levels of success. An institutional focus is one of the most common characteristics of successful firms.

Discerning Unwritten Rules

3

There are aspects of successful governance that should not be overlooked, and are best identified as *unwritten rules*. There are certain overarching factors that are commonly found in successful firms with positive cultures. Hopefully, writing them down for this discussion isn't a serious breach of their intrinsic nature.

Rule 1: Eliminate Internal Competition

Lawyers should focus their energies on competing in the marketplace. Any competitive spirit needs to be directed outward and not between or among individual lawyers within the firm, which puts the lawyers' energies in the wrong place. Unfortunately, too many firms exhibit excessive levels of internal competition, often as a result of the partner compensation system.

As part of the governance process, firm leaders need to look at the extent of internal competition among its lawyers and evaluate the harmful consequences of that focus. In most cases, the conclusion will be that internal competition is consuming time and energy that could be better spent focusing externally to be more competitive in the marketplace. The objective should be to focus the lawyers on making the firm successful as an institution, rather than on each lawyer trying to outdo the others.

Rule 2: Value the Team Player

Successful firms find a way to appropriately value a team player's contributions. In a profession where egos can be large and lawyers seek to promote and publicize their own individual successes, rewarding team players can be a challenge. Although it is sometimes difficult to appreciate the value of team players, egotistical lawyers tend to ignore their overriding responsibility to advance the firm's interests.

While direct financial productivity has to be appropriately recognized, it should not be at the complete expense of the firm's team players who provide both the glue and commitment to the firm which are essential ingredients for success. Whatever the compensation system, the importance of team players should be recognized.

Rule 3: Confront Sacred Cows

A *sacred cow* is an activity, a practice or a behavior of an individual, who gets away with ignoring firm policy or procedures. Often, the *sacred cow* is a senior partner, someone associated with a senior partner, or a strong performer. In past times, firms ignored *sacred cows* and worked around them.

Governance was troublesome because managers had to promote firm policy with some partners, while others got away with violating the policies. *Sacred cows* are unhealthy under the best of circumstances, but they can be deadly in a struggling firm. Stop ignoring the *sacred cows* and take action.

Rule 4: Expose Secret Agendas

Secret agendas are a partner's undisclosed motives whose positions and arguments in firm matters do not reveal the individual's real goal. When arguing head-to-head over an administrative issue, other past or current disputes may be the underlying motivation for one or both individuals to take inflexible positions on the issue at hand. Secret agendas undercut good governance and should be exposed for candid and productive discussions.

Rule 5: Cleanse the Firm of Disruptive Personalities

Almost every firm has a partner who is disruptive to the firm's orderly operation and is tolerated due to senior status or high productivity. One "bad apple" . . . you know the rest.

Many firms weigh the pros and cons of confronting a disruptive partner and then end up compromising their standards for one reason or another. Some of these compromises may seem unavoidable, but many firms remain troubled and their possible success stagnated as a result of avoiding the issue rather than facing a tough decision.

Rule 6: Promote Senior Partner Generosity

The generosity of the firm's most productive senior partner is typical in successful firms. That generosity can be exhibited in a variety of ways, but often involves quietly giving up dollars in the income allocation process to provide adequate compensation for the firm's younger members who will likely be tomorrow's high performers. If the partners at the top are exhibiting a generous spirit, rather than fighting for every last dollar, they will be able to build a stronger firm, as well as set a positive example which will permeate all layers of the firm's culture.

Rule 7: Give Change a Chance

The most successful law firms are those that have implemented changes in their practice method as necessary to meet the challenges of the current legal marketplace. For those firms that do not embrace change, the struggle for profitability becomes harder with each passing year. For many firms, change comes only when its very existence is threatened. For some, the revelation comes too late.

Leading Your Firm to a Better Future

The law firms in the most trouble these days are the firms that have a lack of leadership, suffer from dysfunctional governance, or both. Let there be no mistake about it: Governance is important. Although the subject may not be taught in law school, law publications give it minimal treatment, and it doesn't get the attention of topics like billings and collections, it plays a critical role in the law firm's overall success. Yet, this fact is often under-appreciated by lawyers who consider it a necessary evil and not worthy of a great deal of concern or effort. Most lawyers give it low priority.

Successful law firms provide good client service, are financially healthy, and have strong partner relationships. Keeping firms on track involves paying attention to governance issues, making improvements as necessary, and avoiding any decline in governance processes. For firms with financial or relationship issues, it is likely that governance issues are no small part of the problem.

Part II presents summary discussions of the critical topics and lays the foundation for Part III, a step-by-step approach to improving your firm's governance.

Partner Relations 4

Without an adequate written agreement, law firms are waiting for trouble to strike. Healthy partner relationships are based on mutual respect and, most important, a comprehensive written agreement. If the written agreement is overlooked due to the everyday pressures of a law practice, a controversy eventually will emerge that saps the firm's vitality and success, or worse. Now is the time to put the partnership house in order.

Law Firm Entity Structures

The traditional partnership structure has served lawyers well over time. The partnership format has given way to other entity structures, however, including professional associations and limited liability partnerships. These new choices for lawyers are the result of state legislation allowing lawyers to practice in these differing entity structures.

In the 1970s, professional associations were authorized by many state legislatures to give lawyers their first alternative to the traditional partnership arrangement. Professional associations are corporate-type entities and were attractive to lawyers because they eliminated joint and several liability and allowed lawyers to take advantage of certain tax advantages previously allowed only to business corporations. Many law firms switched to professional associations in the 1970s only to find that many of the tax advantages have now been eliminated.

Limited liability companies for lawyers (sometimes called limited liability partnerships) emerged in the 1990s, again the result of state legislative action. These entities allowed lawyers to take advantage of limited liability while retaining the tax advantages of a partnership. Since there can be adverse tax ramifications associated with terminating a professional association, lawyers continue to practice in professional associations, even though many of the tax reasons for electing that form of entity have been eliminated.

Partnerships

There are two basic advantages to the partnership form: flexibility and taxes. The partnership form provides the greatest flexibility and easily accommodates changes in the partnership ranks, as well as mergers and other re-arrangements. The partnership has to submit a federal tax return, but the taxable income is passed through to the partners, who are taxed at their individual rates.

The most significant disadvantage of a partnership involves joint and several liability. Under this partnership form, each partner is jointly and severally liable for the actions or obligations of the partnership and any one of its partners acting under the partnership.

In today's market, new law firms are rarely organized as a traditional partnership. A few lawyers, however, continue to believe in the traditional form of partnering and do not want to be perceived in the community to be overly focused on avoiding responsibility for their actions. In their view, the words "limited liability" as part of a law firm name may not be helpful in building client confidence.

Professional Associations

When legislatures authorized lawyers to practice in professional associations, many partnerships switched to professional associations because of:

- *Limited liability.* The lawyers are employees of a professional association and are protected from the liabilities of the company and the actions of other lawyers with whom they practice.
- *Tax advantages.* There have been substantial tax advantages relating to the deductibility of fringe benefits, many of which have now been eliminated by subsequent tax legislation.

Disadvantages of the corporate form:

- *Difficulty shifting shares.* Stock transactions of the shareholders may be complex as percentage interests in the firm change over time.
- *Lack of flexibility.* Mergers involving professional associations, particularly in different jurisdictions, may present complexities.
- *Tax issue.* By practicing in the corporate entity, lawyers are subject to a claim of unreasonable compensation in connection with high salaries or bonuses, which could result in the double taxation of dividend treatment if successfully challenged by the IRS.

There are a number of reasons why many lawyers practicing in professional associations have not made the shift to a limited liability company structure, including the costs involved or possible adverse tax ramifications, making the possibility of change either expensive or of marginal value.

Limited Liability Companies

State legislatures now provide for lawyers to operate in limited liability companies (LLCs). Although the exact name of the entity varies from state to state (limited liability partnership, limited liability company, etc.), the concept is similar in each jurisdiction: The advantages of LLCs are:

- Limited liability
- The tax treatment advantages of a partnership

While most lawyers are adopting this new structure for their law firms, there is a cautionary message that needs to be understood. No court has yet ruled upon the limited liability aspects of these entities in a case brought by a client who has been harmed by a lawyer's negligence. Commentators speculate on whether the court would side with the lawyers and against an injured client.

Two-Tier Partnerships

The two-tier partnership emerged in the 1980s when many firms found they had been overly generous in their offers of partnership. The concept that involves equity and non-equity partners applies equally to professional associations and limited liability companies.

Many firms found themselves with younger partners who were still operating in a subordinate role, thereby diluting the profits available to the *real* partners. The two-tier system provides law firms an ability to manage the partnership growth and have more time to evaluate the candidates for equity partnership.

Under a two-tier partnership, the second tier is made up of non-equity partners who are not responsible for a buy-in, are salaried, and have no opportunity to share in the profits except for the possibility of an employee-like merit bonus. In some cases, the two-tier partnership provides a process that allows associates to be elevated to partnership earlier in their careers than otherwise would be the case. In other situations, the two-tiered partnership provided a permanent non-equity position for the associate. The non-equity partner position may be preferable to a strict *up-or-out* policy.

The non-equity partners often participate in some portion of the management function. While the more significant decisions are reserved for the equity partners, the firm can be structured so that the non-equity partners participate in firm management and other routine decisions required by the firm.

Does a Two-Tier Partnership Make Sense?

It depends. Small firms rarely have two-tier partnerships as they find them unnecessary and too cumbersome. For larger firms, two-tier partnerships may make sense in the following circumstances:

- When there is pressure on the firm to offer partnerships before the firm has had an adequate opportunity to evaluate the associate's performance
- When there is pressure on the firm to offer partnerships before the associates have satisfied all of the requirements of a full partner
- To avoid a dilution of equity or profits
- To avoid or delay the buy-in commitment
- To provide more time to evaluate an associate's performance
- To provide a position for lawyers with valuable skills, but who will never meet the qualifications for equity partner
- To provide an alternative to the *up-or-out* standard
- To provide a position for lawyers who, for lifestyle reasons, do not want the obligations that go along with being an equity partner
- To assist lawyers in impressing clients with the title of "partner"

How Does It Work?

The opportunity for second-tier positions of "junior partners," "income partners," or "non-equity partners" may come at an earlier stage in the lawyer's career. The criteria for elevation to non-equity partner will be less stringent than the criteria for equity partner.

Non-equity partners are usually salaried and may be entitled to a bonus similar to that given to associates and staff. They usually have employment agreements that address conditions of termination and other routine employment issues. Non-equity partners are often included in management roles and meetings regarding major decisions, such as setting compensation limited to the equity partners.

Document the Agreement

Regardless of the entity structure determined to be appropriate, the agreement of the owners needs to be documented. While the substantive provisions of the agreement will likely be similar, the format will vary depending on the entity structure.

- *Partnership.* The only necessary document is the partnership agreement.
- *Professional association.* Typically, articles of agreement are filed with the State to create the entity. The substantive operating provisions are set out in the by-laws. In addition there may be stock purchase agreements and employment agreements.
- *Limited liability companies.* Articles of agreement create the entity. The members of the limited liability company enter into an operating agreement that includes the operating provisions.

If lawyers in small and mid-sized firms were graded on the quality of their work documenting their own law firm agreements, there would be a lot of "Ds" for dismal, exceeded only by the majority who would score an "I" for incomplete. These are the same lawyers who would not allow their clients to buy a bicycle without better documentation.

Typically, small firms are started with a handshake between friends. Benefiting from the enthusiasm for the new venture, the new partners overlook the possibility of any future controversy or failure. But give the lawyers some credit; one of the partners is likely to be assigned the chore of drafting an agreement. And, about half the time, the lawyer assigned the task does come up with a first draft that gets circulated. The firm grows with additional partners joining the rank. Later, when a threatening issue strikes the firm, perhaps decades later, the partners wish the incomplete unsigned agreement languishing in the bottom drawer had been pushed to completion.

The demonstrated mobility of lawyers in recent years creates a compelling case for a carefully crafted agreement. Lawyers with inadequate agreements are learning hard lessons, both in court and outside the court system.

A Flexible Structure that Anticipates Bad Events

Depending on the type of entity, the critical provisions are found in the partnership agreement, the bylaws, or the operating agreement. For ease of discussion, further references will be to partnership agreements.

Starting with basic concepts, the agreement should create a structure that provides flexibility and anticipates bad events. Flexibility means creating a living document that will provide guidance under changing circumstances. For example, the agreement should anticipate all of the circumstances involved in the admission of new partners, even if that does not seem to be a priority concern to the founding partners.

In addition to its flexibility, the agreement should address the partners' duties and responsibilities when bad events occur. The partners need to think about the range of possibilities, including death, disability, withdrawal, termination, and dissolution. These topics are critical, even if they don't naturally come to mind when lawyers are caught up in the enthusiasm of starting a new venture.

Critical Provisions

The most critical issues that should be addressed in every partnership agreement are:

- *Partners.* Who are the partners? What is the process for inviting lawyers to become partners in the future?
- *Capital.* What is the amount of startup capital contributed by each of the original partners? How are the capital accounts maintained? What will be the capital contribution expected of partners invited to join the firm in the future? Are the future capital contributions determined in the initial agreement or are they the subject of future decisions?
- *Voting.* What are the voting rights of the partners? Equal votes? Weighted votes? To what extent will a majority vote carry an issue? What issues will require a supermajority vote?
- *Profits.* How are the profits to be divided among the partners? Is it based on a formula system, a subjective system, a combination of both, or some other system? Is the process of dividing profits set forth in detail in the partnership agreement or is it delegated to the partners as a matter of policy which can more easily be changed from time to time?
- *Management.* How is the firm to be managed? What management responsibilities are delegated to a management committee or a managing partner? What management issues are retained by the partners? To what extent is the management plan specified in the partnership agreement?
- *Retirement.* What happens when a partner elects to retire? What are the rights of the partner and what are the obligations of the partnership?

- *Disability.* What happens if one of the partners becomes disabled? What happens if there is a dispute as to whether a partner is disabled? How long will the firm continue to pay compensation to the disabled partner? How does one define the difference between a temporary disability and a permanent disability?
- *Death.* What happens if a partner dies? Are there any death benefits? Is the estate entitled to a payment representing the deceased's ownership interest in the firm? How is the interest of a deceased partner valued for these purposes? Or, alternatively, does the estate only receive a return of the deceased partner's capital?
- *Withdrawal.* What happens when a partner decides to withdraw from practicing with the firm? How much notice is required? How is the firm's interest protected? What monies is the withdrawing partner entitled to receive? Capital account? A share of the value of the firm? How is that determined? What is the process for notifying clients of the intended withdrawal? What does the letter say to the clients of the withdrawing partners? Who sends out the letters?
- *Expulsion.* What are the rights of the partnership to terminate a partner? What are the grounds? What behaviors would trigger an automatic termination? Disbarment? Suspension? Personal bankruptcy? What behaviors would represent cause for discretionary termination, if so voted by the partners? Does the termination of a partner require a supermajority vote?
- *Liquidation.* What are the rights and responsibilities of the partners after a vote to liquidate?

Partnership Criteria

Developing and communicating the criteria for partnership is critical to the orderly succession within the firm and the morale of your associates. What does it take to become a partner in the firm? Do you know the answer? Do your associates know the answer? How do you answer that question during the recruiting process?

Ownership Mentality

The world is full of bright young lawyers who have no clue as to what it takes to be a successful lawyer. A lawyer with an employee mentality will not make a good partner. To be successful, a partnership needs to be made up of individuals who have an entrepreneurial spirit and a concern about contributing to the success of the organization. Clients are not a given. Profits are not assured. Associates who are candidates for partner need to be exposed to these ownership concerns and they need to be evaluated as potential partners based upon whether they "get it."

What Is a Partner?

A partner is a lawyer who has been elevated to an ownership position within a law firm. A partner should be the lawyer who has graduated from the role of subordinate worker and accepted the responsibilities of ownership, which includes contributing to the overall success of the firm by attracting business not only for oneself but for others in the firm.

The offer of partnership may be based on a variety of factors; however the standard is lax in some law firms, as associates are elevated to partner after six or so years, provided they haven't caused a serious problem. This type of liberal standard is responsible for many firms that became partner heavy during the 1980s and 1990s.

Partnership Criteria

Partnership criteria needs to be adopted by the partners and communicated to the associates and candidates interviewing with the firm. In developing the criteria, firms often begin with an introductory paragraph which references accepting the responsibilities of partnership and is followed by a list of the criteria. Common provisions may include:

- Minimum period of time in the practice of law
- Minimum period of time with the firm
- High quality of legal work
- High ethical standards
- Ability to develop a self-sustaining practice
- Commitment to marketing
- Adherence to firm policies and a contributor to a positive culture
- Contributions to the management of the firm
- Serves a need within the law firm

Leadership and Management 5

Strong leadership and effective management can make the difference in a law firm's success. Some firms start out with one or more founding partners who provide the strong leadership that propels the firm to success. The firm's reputation is tied directly to the founders' personalities and talents.

Ironically, it is likely that the stronger the founding partners, the greater the leadership void in the next generation of lawyers. The same firm may flounder and lack direction decades later when the founder or first generation of lawyers retires. In many situations, these firms split apart leaving the second generation of lawyers to look for career opportunities elsewhere.

Other firms may be composed of partners who are successful practitioners, but lack the skills or the inclination to become the firm's leaders. These firms struggle to provide some level of individual success for each lawyer, but have difficulty moving the firm to the next level. The lack of leadership prevents the group of individual lawyers from emerging as a stronger and a more financially healthy firm. The firm does not provide career opportunities for younger lawyers and the firm has no choice but to wind down as the strong performers phase out of the practice.

Eventually, successful firms establish strong leadership, mentoring and a succession plan. These firms continue to grow and will endure from one generation of lawyers to the next. Clients have the opportunity to have their legal needs addressed by an evolving firm. Older lawyers have the support of younger lawyers to assist them as they seek to reduce their workload and proceed to a senior status. Retiring from an ongoing firm provides senior lawyers with a platform from which to phase out effectively, with some level of continuing contact and firm benefits.

For mature firms without a natural leader, developing or finding an individual to fill the role becomes a difficult, but critical challenge.

Leadership, Leadership, Leadership

A leader of a law firm is the person who, by words, actions and example, can articulate the firm's vision and inspire others to follow the lead. Leading is more than being a successful lawyer. Leading is more than managing. Leading is more than being a cheerleader. Effective leaders inspire confidence and motivate others to take the actions necessary to achieve the firm's vision.

Book after book has been written on the topic of leadership, but those books written in the context of corporate America are not specific to that of leadership in the legal context. Lawyers are uniquely an assemblage of autonomy-loving professionals and normally do not react well to taking directions from others. Faced with this formidable challenge, how do we find lawyers who are capable of and willing to provide necessary leadership for our firms?

What Is Leadership?

There are many aspects to leadership, but let's focus on some core concepts. A leader needs to:

- Have a vision
- Be able to identify the goals and objectives necessary to achieve that vision
- Be able to communicate the vision to partners, associates and staff
- Bring about buy-in to the vision and the actions necessary to achieve the vision
- Be able to motivate others to employ behaviors designed to achieve the goals and objectives of the firm
- Be an advocate for the firm's values and a positive influence on the firm's culture
- Engender respect and confidence by members of the firm

Law Firm Leadership

Now, let's go back to our assemblage of autonomous professionals who, in the context of the law firm, needs leaders.

Most successful lawyers have some general leadership qualities which they exhibit in client matters, community activities, and in social and family matters. At the same time, practicing lawyers tend to be set in their ways and unwilling to follow others with a different view than theirs. Simply put, they don't like being told what to do or how to do it. As a result, law firm leadership confronts challenges far more complex than those faced by corporate leaders who work in an environment with more direct lines of authority.

The law firm leader needs to be:

- Perceived as an individual who always subordinates personal interests to the more important cause of advancing the firm's success
- Perceived as objective and free from bias or any agendas other than the firm's success as an institution
- Non-political in the law firm context, not being perceived as an advocate for any particular individuals or practice groups
- Trusted by others as objective, fair minded, and even handed

Law Firm Management

Management is different than leadership. Managers carry out and implement the policies established by the firm's owners. Management has limited discretion and is involved in the day-to-day issues of running the law firm.

Effective managers need different skills than leaders. A person can be a great manager and an ineffective leader. Or, alternatively, a person can be a great leader and a lousy manager. With the exception of small firms, most law firms are led by a managing partner or an executive committee (sometimes called management committee) and are managed by an administrator.

If the firm has an administrator, as do most firms with ten or more lawyers, make certain that the administrator's makeup is compatible with the firm's culture. Too often, the administrator's role of enforcing policy has a tough policing component, which can have a negative effect if not handled well. On the other hand, the administrator can be tough, fair and well respected and a positive influence on the firm's culture.

Understand the difference between leadership and management and make certain that your firm has strong leaders leading and effective managers managing. Having made the distinction, it is necessary to note that for purposes of the next discussion, management models commonly include both leadership and management.

Management Models

The law firm's management structure tends to evolve over time, starting from the day the firm is founded. The older the firm, the more likely it has progressed through several stages. Depending on a variety of circumstances, any of the stages may have application today. Firms re-evaluating their management structure may want to consider moving to the next phase in what is seen as a normal progression.

Founder

At the inception of every law firm, one of the founders typically takes over the leadership of the new firm. This leader operates as a benevolent dictator, making the decisions and taking complete control. The leader's power is derived from a combination of inherent abilities and perceived success in leading the firm. This model usually continues until the leader approaches retirement, at which point the next generation of partners begins to recognize a need for someone to replace the founder in leading the firm.

Democracy in Action

When a firm operates under the leadership of a benevolent dictator for an extended period of time, the next generation of lawyers may have become disenfranchised, which will give rise to a strong desire for more of a say in the firm's operation. This results in a transition toward a more democratic form of governance. While deciding a wide range of issues around the partnership table may be the ultimate in inefficiency, the goal of giving all partners an equal say is achieved. This model may seem to work well for a period of time, but the inefficiencies of all partners involved in management become obvious.

Management Committee

Faced with a departing founder who has led the firm, most firms evolve to a three-member executive committee with staggered three-year terms as the first step in broadening management involvement. Some firms hold onto the concept that all partners should be candidates for the executive committee, rotating partners on and off over time. Other firms limit participation on the executive committee to those partners who have the ability and the interest to serve in that role.

The chair of the executive committee is typically the person who was in the last year of the three-year term. Meetings can be held once a week or twice a month with reports to the full partners at either monthly or quarterly partnership meetings. The extent of the role of the executive committee members will depend on whether the firm has a qualified administrator to do the legwork and implement the committee's decisions. Without an administrator, the extent of the work can be far-reaching and varied.[1] With an administrator, the roles of the committee members can be limited to making decisions and handling some of the more sensitive issues.

A committee approach is often necessary following a founder who has operated with centralized power. In that situation, it is healthier to have several lawyers become educated and engaged in managing the firm. Spreading out the responsibility will give a broader group of lawyers with an appreciation of the leadership responsibilities of a law firm.

Managing Partner

The executive committee approach has its own inefficiencies which often leads firms to conclude that they should move to the managing partner model. This move usually comes when the partners recognize that running a law firm is not easy and that one partner should be responsible for developing the necessary expertise and dedicating a significant portion of their time to leading the firm.

Not every partner is suitable for the managing partner role. In fact, very few partners have the inclination, the skills. and, most important, their partners' confidence. Some firms are prevented from moving to the managing partner model because they lack an appropriate candidate. The person selected as managing partner must have a unique set of qualifications that is rarely found in practicing lawyers.

The process comes full circle. The managing partner is akin to the founder but with some subtle differences. They are both single individuals wielding a substantial amount of power within the law firm. While the founder's power is inherent based on status, the managing partner's power must be earned and maintained.

Managing partners may spend anywhere from a quarter of their time to all of their time on management responsibilities, depending on the firm's size. As a result, managing partners, by necessity, have to scale back their practice and give up clients or not pursue new clients. Managing partners

---

[1]In that circumstance, the committee is sometimes referred to as a management committee, signifying a more hands-on role.

need to be compensated fairly for their time and effort in managing the firm and need to be protected from the day when they no longer will be managing the firm and will be left to face a diminished law practice.

Law firms need to evaluate their present management structure and consider allowing it to evolve to a more efficient and effective stage. With changing times, it has become increasingly necessary for law firms to make and implement decisions quickly. Centralized management should be the ultimate goal, with an eye on preserving as much lawyer time as possible for billable work.

Practice Groups

As law firms grow beyond ten lawyers, practice groups are formed to manage the methods of delivering legal services in each of the practice areas. Because of the general practice nature of the smallest firms, these practice groups may originate in the first instance as the Litigation Practice Group and the Non-Litigation Practice Group. As the firm grows, four or five practice groups are likely to emerge, such as Estate Planning Practice Group, Probate Practice Group, Real Estate Practice Group, Business Law Practice Group, and Litigation Practice Group. The larger firms may have from ten to fifteen practice groups, depending upon the practices of the lawyers within the firm.

The primary role of a practice group is to provide a structure for managing the lawyers, paralegals, and staff who are providing client services in a particular area of the law. A practice group is led by a practicing lawyer with leadership and administrative skills. Meetings are held periodically, perhaps once a month. The practice group should address the following topics:

- Changes in the law
- Quality control
- Forms and systems
- Case selection
- Fee agreements
- Resources, technology
- Workload distribution, staffing, training
- Billing practices
- Collections

Much of the work of practice groups is related to the substantive law and delivery of client services. In recent years, however, there has been a growing need for practice group leaders serving firm management to be responsible for predicting and managing the production of revenue.

The Law Firm Administrator

Managing a law firm involves practice management and business management. As previously noted, most firms have practice groups that handle issues relating to how law is practiced and how services are delivered to clients. Business management, on the other hand, involves many of the day to day responsibilities of running a business. There is no need for lawyers to spend time on business management when there is an entire profession of legal administrators trained to deal with those issues. The law firm administrator should be delegated the business management functions after the policies have been set by the partners, the executive committee, or the managing partner.

Small Firms

Most firms, even the small ones, have someone in the administrative role. For example, in a three-lawyer firm the administrative duties are often carried out on a part-time basis by the firm's most experienced secretary. By the time the firm reaches ten lawyers, it can probably justify a full-time administrator with a solid business background. The qualifications and credentials of the individual serving as administrator increase with the size of the firm, as does the level of authority delegated. The administrator relieves the lawyers of many time-consuming matters and preserves the lawyers' time for billable work and, hopefully, is better positioned than the lawyers to apply good business principles to the firm resulting in increased profits.

Large Firms

Law firm administrators are essential in larger firms. It is a full-time role that often involves the supervision of administrative support personnel. In the largest firms, the administrator is sometimes called the executive director, a position that carries a salary which is equal to a mid-level partner.

In large firms, there will be a team of individuals supervised by the administrator. The team might include:

- Accountant/bookkeeper
- Technology and information resources specialist
- Human resources manager
- Librarian
- Marketing director
- Paralegal manager

With good support to handle the day-to-day management functions, the executive director is free to serve the partners directly, assisting with policy decisions, long-range planning, and support for the efforts of the practice groups.

Financial Challenges 6

These are great times to be a lawyer. At least, that is how the saying goes. Perhaps it would be more accurate to say these are "the best of times and the worst of times." Opportunities are unlimited and some firms are reaching levels of unparalleled success. But there is another side to the story. Some firms struggle to survive due to unresolved financial challenges. For those firms, time to take remedial action may be short. This chapter explores those challenges in an effort to better define the problems.

Trends Affecting Lawyers

Some trends in the profession are undeniably disturbing. Let's take a look at what we have been seeing in recent years:

Shifts in Client Base

National and international corporations no longer seek out separate outside counsel in every state. Those corporations have contributed to the rise in mega-firms and a shift in the client base of local firms that previously serviced those clients. Local law firms that do not recognize the need to make adjustments in light of the shift in client base are at risk of decline and eventual demise.

Increasing Competition

The number of lawyers has been on the rise, resulting in less good work available for some lawyers. But, more disturbing is the fact that other professionals are encroaching on what has traditionally been considered lawyer's turf. Accounting firms, title companies, and banks are all getting a piece of what used to belong to the legal profession. Multi-disciplinary practice, although not approved by the ABA or allowed under the Rules of Professional Conduct in most states, is creeping into the profession and beginning to have an impact on lawyers.

Expecting More for Less

Clients expect lawyers to be productive and efficient in the delivery of legal services. Hours worked no longer justify the legal fee. Lawyers must provide value for the dollars clients spend. Sophisticated clients scrutinize the value of hours billed and hire auditors to review their lawyer's bills

Pressure on Hourly Rates

A law firm can no longer simply increase its rates to produce needed revenue. Most hourly rates are about as high as they can go without pricing the lawyers out of the market. An oversupply of lawyers means there is always someone there ready to do the work for a lower price.

Increasing Costs

Technology, advertising, health insurance, associate salaries, etc., are among the law firm costs that have impacted the bottom line in recent years.

Decline in Law Firm Cultures

Law firm cultures are in decline. A growing emphasis on quality of life has caused lawyers to question the demands of the profession. The loyalty of partners, associates, and staff to the law firm seems to be in decline. Lateral movement between firms is on the increase, as are departures from the profession.

These trends are creating challenges for many law firms. The solutions of the past no longer work. Under these circumstances, the first step is to implement some improved, but traditional, management concepts. The second step is to prepare your lawyers to think about more fundamental changes in the business of practicing law. Keep in mind that many success stories are based on lawyers facing up to major changes in the profession that require embracing a new paradigm.

Budgeting

Let's start with a discussion of a routine process called budgeting. In most firms, the administrator has the responsibility for creating the budget that includes both revenue expectations and anticipated expenses. Many firms focus only on expenses, leaving revenue to chance. The real challenge of budgeting in law firms is how to project the revenues that will be produced by the lawyers. The expense side is the easy part.

Two different approaches can be used. One approach is for the administrator to consult with each lawyer to discuss his or her revenue expectations in the coming year. With that approach, the administrator is relying upon the high hopes of individual lawyers. The administrator has the opportunity to insert a lower number into the firm revenue budget, but at the same time the administrator may not want to interfere with the lawyer's commitment to achieve a certain revenue result.

The other way to go about projecting revenue is for the administrator to derive the individual revenue expectations from a formula approach. Based on past performance, the administrator projects the realistic billable hour expectations of each lawyer and multiplies the number times the hourly rate and then applies a percentage discount to cover anticipated write downs and collection problems. Both approaches have serious shortcomings, but there are no better ways to project revenue.

Here is the central point. Budgeting includes revenue planning. The extension of this discussion involves recognizing that each lawyer should focus on revenue improvement as a part of the overall budget discussion. If your firm does not include a significant discussion of revenue, consider revamping the firm's whole budgeting process.

Budgets for law firms seem basic, but many firms fail to conduct an effective budgeting process. A surprising number of smaller firms use the check book approach; that is, check the account balance and then make a decision on an expense or a purchase. Other firms become hostage to the past by looking only at changes to the budget, thereby institutionalizing all prior expense items. And, too many firms do not work to manage the revenue side of the budget, thereby leaving cash flow completely to chance.

An effective budgeting process is guided by the following rules:

Rule 1: Sign the checks.

At least, do it for a month. There is no better way to understand where the money goes. Managing partners who limit their role to reviewing P&L statements and supervising a bookkeeper become removed from the process. Signing the checks can be an awakening for lawyers who have positioned themselves too distant from the money.

Rule 2: Be on the lookout for excessive and unnecessary spending.

With changes in the marketplace, items that were once essential may no longer be needed. Budgets often have buried deep within them items that were approved in earlier times and not routinely reconsidered.

Rule 3: Do not try to solve all the firm's problems by cutting expenses.

While it is true that excessive spending should be curtailed, most firms are able to bring their expense budget into acceptable form after working at it for a couple of years. Once the fat is gone from the expense budget, the endless search for further cuts can become a matter of diminishing returns. Savings are harder and harder to find, and aggressive cutting can have worse adverse effects, which may lead to undermining both the firm's morale and its productivity.

Think of your costs as fitting into three categories: fixed costs, staff and productivity-related costs, and discretionary costs. For most firms, the largest expense is staff costs, followed by fixed costs and finally discretionary costs which make up only 10 percent to 20 percent of the firm's annual expenses.

Avoid the trap of causing morale problems and loss of revenue by undermining the firm's capacity to produce the necessary work. Don't be like the firm that became so obsessed with reducing expenses that it cut back staff to the point the lawyers became so unproductive the firm went out of business.

Rule 4: Spend more time on the revenue side of the budgeting process than on the expense side.

Too many firms obsess over the expense budget year after year and have little or no time or energy left to address the revenue budget. The annual budgeting process should include working with lawyers individually on their plans for the coming year. This is often done in an evaluation process where the lawyer's prior year's performance is reviewed and commitments are made for the coming year.

The process should focus on hours, realization, marketing, and client development efforts, all of which should result in the lawyer committing to a revenue number for the coming year. Each lawyer should take seriously their revenue responsibility and be accountable for a share of the revenue, as agreed upon during the planning process.

Rule 5: Conduct a zero-based budgeting process every five years.

Zero budgeting means that each item has to be justified before it goes back into the budget. Zero-based budgeting is the best means for finding and eliminating unnecessary expenses that have become institutionalized by the process.

Working with Financial Indicators

Once the budget is in place, there needs to be an effective way to monitor results and adjust behaviors and/or expectations. At the same time, you will probably be looking for opportunities to improve revenue. Make sure you have the following financial indicators on your radar:

Billing Realization Rate

Determine the firm's billing realization rate and then adopt a plan for improvement. A 5 percent increase in billing realization can make a big improvement to the bottom line.

Collection Realization Rate

Determine the firm's collection realization and then adopt a plan for improvement. Again, a 5 percent improvement will make a big difference to the bottom line.

Efficiency of Lawyers and Paralegals

Lawyers and paralegals may need to be more productive during their hours in the office. In many circumstances, better work habits can add billable hours without increasing the length of a working day. By shifting a half-hour each day for each timekeeper from non-billable to billable time, a firm can make a significant increase to its revenue.

Increased Profit Margin

By incrementally shifting away from hourly billing, law firms can achieve higher profit margins on the billable hours invested.

By improving results in any of these areas, the firm is increasing revenue production, not only in the current year, but in each succeeding year, as long as the improved methods of operation continue. But, the analysis does not stop there. The following are two additional areas for improved revenue that can provide one-time gains:

- *Billing turnover rate.* If the firm can improve its billing turnover by fifteen days, the firm can expect a surge of revenue equal to about one-half of the firm's monthly revenue.
- *Collection turnover rate.* If the firm can improve the average collection time by fifteen days, it can expect a surge of revenue equal to about one-half of a month's revenue.

Unlike the realization rates, the extra revenue flow from an improvement in turnover rates will represent a one-time surge of revenue.

Each financial indicator can be tracked on a firm basis, a practice group basis, or on an individual basis. A full set of financial reports can result in too much data for the average practicing lawyer. For the data to be meaningful, it needs to be condensed preferably to one page that provides a snapshot for the practicing lawyers.

Sources of Capital

Capital can be a challenge for law firms. Only lawyers can invest and the result, not surprisingly, is that law firms tend to be under-capitalized. Resorting to lines of credit from local banks is typical, particularly for law firms struggling with cash flow problems.

Most firms start up with a modest investment from its founders and a line of credit from a bank as soon as the firm can satisfy the requirement for collateral. Following the start-up investment, firms may need additional capital from time to time to even out cash flow and/or to support growth. In some firms, new partners are required to buy in and those new funds are used to increase the capital of the firm. However, these sources of money do little to change the overall under-capitalization of most law firms.

Money Sources Available to Law Firms

- *Partner investment.* Partners may be expected to contribute capital to the firm upon their admission as a partner or at any future time when by a vote of the partners a determination is made that further contributions of capital are necessary in order to fund a particular situation.
- *Bank borrowing.* Gone are the days when a bank will loan money to a law firm without collateral. Bank money is available, if the firm is willing to collateralize the loan with its assets, including receivables. As a practical matter, that means that startup law firms have to fund the first thirty to sixty days with the partners' capital investment. Most banks require that the law firm pay down its line of credit for a period of at least thirty days in each fiscal year.
- *Equipment lease.* Law firms are able to lease their computers and other equipment as a means of avoiding the capital requirement for a straight purchase.
- *Retained earnings.* The firm can increase its capital by retaining and not distributing all of the profits of the law firm during a given year. Because of the constant desire for distributable cash, this is

not a popular approach in most firms. Further, from a tax stand-point, retaining earnings involves after-tax dollars.

■ *Partner loans.* One or more partners can make a loan to the firm to fund a particular situation. The interest paid on these loans can be at a favorable rate. Law firms differ on whether these loans should be compulsory and on a pro rata basis or voluntary. If they are voluntary, the partners who do loan money to the firm could be in a position of increased power. A few firms have allowed loans to be voluntary but have kept the identity of the individuals loaning money confidential, with the exception of the managing partner, administrator, and bookkeeper.

■ *Loans from relatives.* Anyone can loan money to a law firm. Few are willing to do that, so the marketplace may be narrowed to loans from relatives of the partners.

■ *Credit cards.* Forgive the mention of credit cards. It is included in a list of sources of money, not because it is a reasonable idea but simply because an increasing number of law firms are resorting to credit card borrowing as a funding mechanism. Don't do it.

Preparing Your Firm for the Future

A focus on the following factors will position your firm to take the bolder steps necessary to remain competitive in the changing marketplace.

■ *Develop a vision.* Without a unified direction, the firm will be nothing more than a number of lawyers with individual agendas heading in different directions. No firm can be successful without a common vision.

■ *Centralize management.* Centralized management gives a firm an ability to move quickly and take bolder steps in reacting to the needs of its clients. Consensus driven firms will not be able to keep up with the necessary changes and will fall behind the competition.

■ *Expand the role of non-lawyers.* By shifting a larger portion of the work to qualified paralegals, lawyers are able to provide better service at a lower cost, while maintaining or increasing firm profits. This trend will continue as clients resist having all the work performed at lawyer rates.

■ *Focus on value to the client.* There has been a complete shift in the pricing of legal services. Clients are no longer content with price based solely on the time invested by the lawyer. Every service has an intrinsic value to the client. Now, price needs to be based on the client's perception of value, with the lawyer having the challenge of producing the service at a profit.

- ***Improve budgeting and forecasting.*** Lawyers need to improve their ability to budget and forecast the cost of their services. While there are uncertainties unique to the law business, lawyers can learn from the planning and budgeting methods of contractors who are required to submit bids on proposed projects.
- ***Be prepared to take risks.*** Hourly rate billing allocates all of the risk to the client. In the years ahead, lawyers who are prepared to share risk with the client will have a competitive advantage.
- ***Become client driven.*** Clients are more mobile than in the past and will not be loyal to lawyers who fail to meet their expectations. Excellent client service includes meaningful involvement in planning, predictable fees and effective communication throughout the project.

Revenue Opportunities

7

The vast majority of law firms leave money on the table—that is, there are places where revenue can be improved easily. Once you have the financial indicators under control and set goals for incremental improvements, the next question involves what changes can be made to achieve those goals.

Revenue Focus

A common failing is focusing on cost reduction to the exclusion of the more meaningful revenue approach. While extravagant and unnecessary spending must be eliminated from the law firm budget, cost cutting has serious limitations. If taken to the extreme, it can undercut the firm's production capacity. No firm has forged its way to long-term success though cost cutting.

On the revenue side, firms that limit their analysis to adjustments in billable hours and hourly rates also make a mistake. While some firms survived the 1990s by regularly increasing billable hour requirements and raising their hourly rates, those strategies are self-limiting over time and, in many cases, have resulted in increased client dissatisfaction and serious decline in lawyer morale.

Here is an important concept: *Increasing revenue, while maintaining the same expense structure, is the most powerful approach to improve the firm's bottom line.* Simple math demonstrates that those extra revenue dollars go straight to the bottom line and make a profound impact on partner profits. If the firm has an expense ratio of 50 percent, an increase in revenues of 10 percent will boost partner profits by 20 percent. The math is quite favorable. If costs can be held constant, those extra dollars can make a big difference in the partners' lifestyle and satisfaction.

Too many firms have already pushed their hourly rates and their hourly production numbers to the limit. Further rate increases may adversely affect client relationships and result in problems attracting new business. Similarly, increasing billable hour requirements of hard-working lawyers and paralegals is not a good idea. The goal is to find places to improve revenue within the existing cost structure that will not adversely impact client relationships or lawyer morale.

Lawyers need to understand that there are both healthy and unhealthy approaches to improving revenue. These recommendations are based on approaches that are consistent with maintaining healthy lawyer/client relationships and a positive law firm environment.

Revenue Capacity

The law firm's revenue capacity is deemed to be the amount of money that the firm should be able to generate with its lawyers and paralegals working at their highest and most efficient level in the context of its existing support, its present systems, and its current technology. It represents the most revenue that the firm might hope for, with its present operating structure and practice methods. The firm's capacity should be used as a benchmark to get a sense of how the firm is doing and the extent to which it has unrealized revenue potential.

Start by taking the standard hourly rate of each lawyer and paralegal and multiply the rate by the anticipated number of billable hours. The hours to be used in the analysis should be realistic based on the firm's size, location, culture, the type of work involved, and, most important, historical information regarding each individual's performance in prior years.

For example:

Lawyer A	1,600 hours x $200	=	$320,000
Lawyer B	1,750 hours x $150	=	$262,500
Paralegal	1,500 hours x $90	=	$135,000
			$717,500 Revenue Capacity

The analysis assumes that the work performed is billed based on hourly rates or, if other billing methods are used, that the hourly rates provide the basis for estimating anticipated revenue. The analysis also assumes that each lawyer and paralegal has an adequate workload, that all billable hours are billed to clients, and that all bills to clients get paid. While these are aggressive assumptions, they do represent the firm's capacity and a decent goal, whether or not it is ever achieved.

Next, compare your firm's revenue capacity to its actual revenue performance. What you have accomplished is to highlight the places which provide opportunity for improvement. Many seemingly hard-working firms are operating at 50 percent or 60 percent of their actual capacity. Moving the percentage up a little as 5 percent to 10 percent will result in a substantial improvement in the firm's profits.

Setting Goals

Once you have examined your firm's financial indicators, consider setting goals for improvement, for example:

- Improve the collection turnover rate by two weeks
- Improve the billing realization by 5 percent
- Improve the collection realization by 5 percent
- Get associates closer to their goals by achieving an additional 50 billable hours
- Get partners closer to their goals by achieving an additional 50 billable hours

Small incremental improvements in each of the categories will combine to make a significant increase in firm profits. Remember, a 10 percent increase in revenue while maintaining the same expenses will increase firm profits by 20 percent.

Law Firm Leveraging

The next step is to look at some law firm leverage concepts. The pyramid structure, that is leveraging with associates, no longer works for most firms. What worked in the 1960s and 1970s just doesn't cut it anymore. Sophisticated clients have recognized that they often don't get good value for their dollars with inexperienced associates. At the same time, they have a renewed enthusiasm for the expertise of the senior partners, and are willing to pay accordingly.

Leveraging Expertise

Ironically, as clients have become less willing to pay to have a matter handled by inexperienced associates, they are more willing to pay high fees for the experienced "go to" lawyers in any particular field. By charging a premium for their expertise, the best lawyers are able to leverage their own experience and wisdom.

Higher Levels of Expertise

While commodity legal work will always be price sensitive, the work of lawyers with high levels of expertise will not be price sensitive. In the present marketplace, the goal for most lawyers should be to develop a reputation in their community for a certain expertise or, better yet, to be the "go to" person for a particular type of matter. Once that status is achieved, lawyers can leverage their own knowledge and wisdom to achieve greater profits.

Value-based Fee Agreement

It is difficult to leverage a lawyer's expertise to best advantage in matters that are billed by the hour. Higher rates can make a difference, but they do not capture the true value of a lawyer's expertise. As a result, lawyers seeking to leverage their expertise to best advantage are exploring and adopting alternative value-based fee methods.

Leveraging Paralegals

While some of the world's largest firms continue to leverage associates, many firms got in trouble with liberal partnership policies that caused firms to become partner heavy. Sophisticated clients, who will pay high hourly rates for the partners, have become increasingly unwilling to pay for the work of inexperienced associates. As a result, leveraging with associates has diminished as a revenue producer for many firms.

The emergence of the paralegal profession has offered an alternative to associate leverage. Associates continue to be important to law firms, but now can be viewed more in their role as the partners of tomorrow.

Properly managed, qualified paralegals are able to help lawyers provide better client service at a lower cost, while at the same time providing improved profits for the law firm. A central component of any paralegal program is the profitability study. It would make no sense to move work to paralegals if the paralegal program was not returning a profit to the firm.

As the paralegal profession was emerging, the practice of law was becoming more difficult and complex. Lawyers have found it necessary to handle a larger volume of work, which produces greater pressures and a higher intensity. There is less time for detail and less time to attend to issues of client comfort. Both the quality of the work and client satisfaction was at risk. While paralegals bring many advantages to the lawyers and their clients, our analysis here will be limited to the use of paralegals in leveraging profits for the law firm.

To take full advantage of the contribution paralegals are making to the delivery of legal services, the supervising lawyer needs to fully understand Rule 5.3 of the Rules of Professional Conduct (Responsibilities Regarding Nonlawyer Assistants), and local rules.

Properly supervised, a qualified paralegal can perform most other tasks in the delivery of legal services that do not include the practice of law. The practice of law is considered to be giving legal advice, charting the direction of a case, engaging in negotiations for a client, taking a deposition or appearing in court for a client, and accepting a client or setting a fee.

Leveraging with Technology

For the law firm, technology is a mixed bag. Law firms struggle to live with it. Law firms can't live without it. Technology managers are forever working with issues of cost justification, implementation, lawyer buy-in, training, and computer crashes. For all the problems, technology has improved many aspects of client service and law firm operations.

Each technological advance makes lawyers more efficient and more cost effective. With increased price competition, law firms that do not take advantage of the technological advances are at a distinct disadvantage.

In the law firm setting, who benefits from technology? If the work is billed by the hour, the answer is simple. The clients benefit. The lawyer receives no direct benefit. For work that is billed on flat fees, it is the lawyer who stands to benefit from improved use of technology. Similarly, lawyers who handle contingency cases will benefit from technology. The problem in most firms is that the vast majority of legal work is still billed by the hour.

Theoretically, additions in overhead should be covered by increased hourly rates. However, in most legal markets competition will not allow rate adjustments to reflect the additional cost of technology. Many firms have given up and are simply accepting technology as a cost of doing business.

There are two management aspects to technology in the law office. First, technology managers need to evaluate the firm's use of technology and eliminate wasted time, effort, and money. The second step is to develop an approach to clients that permits sharing in the rewards of technology.

The real solution is for firms to move away from hourly rate billing and employ alternative billing methods. Hourly billing has come under attack as being unfair to the client and unfair to the lawyer. But, as it relates to the issue of this chapter, hourly billing (by design) eliminates the lawyer from benefiting from technology. Technology costs become an expense item to be covered by the hourly rate. While the investment in technology justifies an increase in rates, the competition in the marketplace does not allow it. The only way to achieve leverage from technology is to detach billing from time entries. If the fees are set on grounds other than time, then productivity advances from technology will be shared by the lawyers.

Client Expectations

We cannot leave the subject of revenue without referencing one last concept that is underrated by most lawyers: client expectations. No other factor is more important to revenue flow than satisfied clients whose expectations are met in all regards. Any failings to establish appropriate expectations at the beginning will result in client dissatisfaction and, ultimately, a disruption or delay in the payments of legal fees. And for those lawyers who are good at setting expectations at the initial client meeting, disappointments along the way can also affect revenue.

Following an initial visit with a lawyer, the client has certain expectations that will guide the client's thinking as the matter proceeds. Hopefully, those expectations will be based on what the lawyer has said during that first meeting. In some cases, however, the expectations will be based on what the client *thought* he or she heard. The better the information and the more realistic the client's expectations, the more successful the lawyer/ client relationship will be and the easier it will be to bill for those services and collect fees in a timely fashion.

A collection problem is a signal that there was a problem at the beginning of the lawyer/client relationship and that a problem at the time of client intake may have been exacerbated by poor client service or unsatisfactory client communications during the process. A client who is well informed, engaged in the process, and who sees the matter proceeding in line with expectations will tend to be more satisfied with the service and more inclined to send a check by return mail.

Properly managing client expectations will result in the improvement of many of the firm's financial indicators, such as billing realization, billing turnover, collection realization, and collection turnover. Improving each of those indicators by a few percentage points can result in significant additional revenue.

The key to avoiding many client problems is to recognize the significance of the client in-take as the most critical communication you will have with the client. Any problems resulting from misunderstandings at that first meeting may not surface until much later in the process. Often they emerge as collection issues at or near the end of the matter.

Client in-take is only the first step, but it establishes critical aspects of the client relationship that will be destined to affect firm revenue and profits. Following the in-take process, client communications become critical, and most particularly in situations where events occur which will affect the client's expectations. Let the client know of any change immediately. Let the client participate in any changes, particularly those that will affect the fee estimate. Never surprise a client with the amount of a bill.

For a more detailed approach to increasing revenue, see my companion book on the subject, *The Lawyer's Guide to Increasing Revenue: Unlocking the Profit Potential of Your Firm* (2004, ABA Law Practice Management).

Partner Accountability | **8**

A collection of individual lawyers doing their own thing will not succeed in the long term. The lawyers' zealous need to practice law with autonomy challenges some of the best law firm leaders and managers and cuts squarely against efforts to develop a cohesive group of lawyers working together to advance the firm as an institution.

Law firms need to establish a shared vision and implement policies designed to achieve their vision. Keeping partners focused on a common direction and making them accountable to firm management is a priority.

The Significance of Partner Accountability

The firm provides support for partners to promote and advance their practice within a group setting. In return, partners must be accountable for implementing the steps necessary to advance the firm's goals.

Revenue Goals

The law firm has an expense budget that must be covered by revenue from the firm's partners. The administrator or the managing partner can exercise control over expenses, but has no direct ability to control revenue. Without individual partner acceptance of the need to meet the budget revenue, the possibility of financial failure looms as an ongoing possibility.

There must be a process in place for management to hold the partners responsible for doing whatever is necessary, individually and collectively, to meet the revenue budget. The mechanism may involve the setting of individual monthly requirements for billable hours or actual revenue. In firms with practice groups, the budgeted revenue can be allocated and the practice group leaders can play an important role in monitoring progress of its members, intervening to take appropriate action in the event of a possible shortfall. Revenue production cannot be left to chance.

Productivity Measurement

A partner's financial productivity involves more than billable hours. Hours mean nothing unless they are converted into billings and then into dollars in the door. But even billings and collections tell only part of the story. Other aspects that are critical to an analysis of partner productivity include:

- *How profitable was the work?* What was the realization rate? How many billable hours were invested? Were all hours billed and collected, or were there write-offs? The profit margin has become recognized as a critical component in any productivity analysis.
- *What magnitude of the firm's resources was needed to produce those dollars?* The investment in a project is partly the billable hours, but also includes staff support and other firm resources. Some projects take very little overhead resources, while other projects may require massive support. While it is not necessary to compile cost figures for the share of routine overhead expenses, a watchful eye needs to be on the lookout for the use of excessive resources when evaluating the profitability of any particular matter or type of work.
- *Has the partner leveraged associates and paralegals?* The most productive partners are those who manage a large book of profitable work through the use of associates and paralegals. Partners who leverage by delegating to others are typically more productive and more valuable to the firm than partners whose contribution is limited to their own billable hours.

The Use of Financial Reports

The ability to keep partners accountable involves managing financial data and publishing reports intended to measure performance and encourage certain behaviors. While large firms have elaborate sets of reports, slicing and dicing the information in every possible way, smaller firms may be guided by the manner in which the bookkeeper utilizes the financial software. Most financial software packages are capable of reporting far more information than most law firms realize.

Financial Software

Some small and mid-sized firms use off-the-shelf financial software rather than having software developed for their specific needs. The critical point to understand is that many small law firms do not take control of the development of useful financial reports, but rather leave control to the inclinations of their bookkeeper.

Typically, bookkeepers in small and midsized law firms, whether part time or full time, may have not had prior law firm experience. Without guidance from lawyers as to the data that would be useful, the bookkeeper is left to decide how to use the software program. Most off-the-shelf legal software has the capacity to report a wide range of information provided the necessary data is input in an appropriate fashion. This additional data will not get in the system unless the managing partner, or management committee, lets the administrator or bookkeeper know of the need for these additional reports. Lawyer involvement is critical in setting up the financial software program.

Sending the Wrong Message

The financial data that is circulated to the partners will send messages that will affect behavior. Here are some common problems which demonstrate how management can send the wrong messages to lawyers:

- **Circulating only billable hours.** If the firm routinely circulates a report showing only the individual billable hours but no other data, the message to the lawyers is that the important factor is booking billable hours. The result is that the lawyers will not treat billings, collections or realization (profitability) as important.
- **Circulating billable hours and the dollar value of the billable hours.** Most software programs make it easy (almost irresistible) to prepare a report that converts billable hours to dollars utilizing standard hourly rates. Unfortunately, these reports allocate dollars to associates and to paralegals. Partners do not get credit for work delegated to associates and paralegals. An unintended consequence is that the exact wrong message is being sent to the partners; that is, if you delegate work you don't get credit for it. Partners, who want to improve their performance on paper, simply stop delegating and do all the work themselves. Another result of this type of reporting is that partners are not held accountable for writing-off associate or paralegal time.
- **Circulating billings and/or collections allocated among partner, associate, and paralegal.** These same reports that allocate dollars to the work of partners, associates, and paralegals also easily break down billings or receipts in the same fashion. The associ-

ates and paralegals can be unfairly judged, because what gets billed and how it is billed is within the province of the partner, as is the collectability of the work taken on. Associates should be judged based on their effort and the quality of their work. Partners should be judged based on their ability to delegate work, manage an increased volume of work, and collect for the work performed.

What to Report and How to Report It

Deciding what to report and how to report should be treated as an important management decision. It takes work and in some cases calls to help lines or consultants engaged to configure the program to produce the desired reports.

Before discussing the data needed to effectively manage the firm, let's start with the concept of sorting the information. In the process, you want the ability to not only provide firm-wide data, but also to sort by both individual lawyers and by practice area. While there may be differences among programs, every client matter needs to be assigned to an individual lawyer and to a practice area. This will allow you to track individuals as well as the performance of each practice area. Any effort to improve firm performance will require an analysis of the data from both perspectives.

Think about the financial data needed to effectively manage a law firm:

Billable Hours by Timekeeper

A Billable Hours Report will permit an evaluation of the number of billable hours of each of the firm's timekeepers. Analyzing where the shortfalls are occurring can help identify workload and practice area issues that need attention. Also, it can identify lawyers or paralegals whose contribution of billable hours may be deficient due to a lack of work, poor work ethic, poor time recording techniques, or inefficient practice methods.

Billings

The Billings Report will demonstrate the dollar value of billings for the month and the total to date for the year. Most firms report billings by partner or by lawyer. It is also useful to sort and evaluate this billings information on a practice group basis. These reports will be useful in assessing each lawyer's productivity and delegation skills, along with the success of each practice group.

Cash

The Cash Report will demonstrate the dollar value of cash collections for the month and the total to date for the year. Cash can be reported for the firm, by partner or by lawyer and by practice group. These reports will be useful in assessing the quality of the clients and the lawyers' success in actually collecting revenue.

Revenue Per Partner

How much revenue each partner is responsible for having produced is important. In addition, average revenue per lawyer is a number that will allow comparisons with industry standards and also help the firm track changes in its productivity from year to year. Some firms track revenue by lawyer; others track revenue by partner. This report can be run either way, or both ways.

Billing Realization Rate

The billing realization rate is the percentage of recorded billable time that gets billed to clients. The amounts that are not billed to clients may have been written off for a variety of reasons. In some cases, it represents time invested that is not well spent; in other situations it is time that cannot be justified based on the intrinsic value of the work or the arrangement with the client. Some lawyers have to write off time due to inefficient work or poor practice methods.

An average billing realization rate for all of the firm's work can be calculated and tracked year to year. A further level of analysis can be conducted by calculating the billing realization rate for a practice area or for an individual lawyer.

Aged Work-in-Process Report

The Aged Work-in-Process Report will show the value of unbilled work as of the date of the report broken down into categories of 30 days, 60 days, 90 days, etc. Some work is billed monthly and other work is billed at conclusion. Obviously the type of work will affect the results. If possible, it is helpful to break down the different types of work into separate reports.

This report will help determine whether there is unbilled work that should have been billed. It can also be used to track the investment of time in matters that are not billed monthly such as flat fee work and contingency work.

Collection Realization Rate

The collection realization rate represents the percentage of billed work that is actually collected. For purposes of this analysis, it is useful to set an arbitrary time period that an unpaid bill will be considered uncollectible. For example, the likelihood of collecting a bill that is over a year old is statistically very low. Carrying uncollectible bills on the accounts receivable report will confuse any financial analysis, and thinking that the money may be collected in the days ahead may give the firm a false sense of well being.

Aged Accounts Receivable Report

The Aged Accounts Receivable Report will show the amounts of unpaid client bill broken down into categories of 30 days, 60 days, 90 days, etc. The Report is used to identify clients with overdue receivables and assess the affect of the firm's collection problem on cash flow.

Subjective Aspects of Productivity

There are aspects of productivity that cannot be measured by objective data. Consider the following contributions:

- *Teamwork.* The partner who is a good team player may be more valuable than the partner who operates as a lone ranger.
- *Training and mentoring.* The training and mentoring of new lawyers and paralegals is critical to the continued success of a law firm. Some partners are generous in their willingness to work with others and that aspect of their work contributes to the productivity of the firm as a whole.
- *Making others more productive.* The true team player is the partner who is more focused on the success of the firm than on their own individual success.

Partner Evaluations

Partner evaluations are utilized by management as one method of holding partners accountable. The process may vary some from firm to firm, but basically each partner's contribution is evaluated based on an annual plan agreed to in the evaluation process a year before.

The evaluation process would start near the end of a calendar year with each partner filling out a Partner Profile Form providing information about the individual's productivity and contribution to the firm during the current year. One member of the Management Committee (or Income Allocation Committee) would meet with each partner to review and discuss the information on the partner profile form.

The full committee would then meet to review the Partner Profile Forms and the results of the individual interviews and create a plan for the coming year giving consideration to contributions needed from each partner to achieve the plan. One member of the committee would then be charged with responsibility to meet with each of the partners to discuss and develop an annual plan for each partner that takes into account the partner's individual interests in the context of the firm goals.

The committee would next craft a narrative description of the strengths of the partner and perceived areas of needed improvement. There would also be a paragraph reflecting the partner's goal for the coming year.

The selected committee member meets with each partner to deliver the evaluation and works with the partner to negotiate an Annual Plan that is consistent with the needs of the firm. The Annual Plan should address changes in practice areas, plans to expand their practice or improve their skills, efforts to train and mentor others, assumption of responsibilities within the firm, any civic or professional participation, and other ways of contributing to the advancement of the goals of the firm. Finally, the plan should include expectations with regard to billable hours, fees billed, and realization achieved. The agreed to plan should be in writing and should be signed by both the partner and the committee member. The annual plan will play a prominent role in the following year's evaluation, as the partner will be reviewed on the basis of whether the commitments in the plan are met.

In a firm with a subjective compensation system, the Annual Plan works well. Achieving the goals set out in the plan would be a significant subjective aspect of the following year's compensation allocation. Even if the firm has a formula compensation system, the Partner Evaluation is important as a direct basis for rewarding or sanctioning good or bad performance. With a formula compensation system, the partners can still promote the annual plan process as a requirement for continued partnership.

Partner Compensation

9

There is no governance issue more important, more delicate, and potentially more destructive than compensation. How partners divide profits likely has it origins in the creation of the firm, perhaps eons ago. This probably means that the system is so entrenched in the firm's culture that any initiative to change the system will be met with resistance rooted in rational or irrational lawyer insecurity.

If your firm is reevaluating its compensation system, the process should be carefully undertaken regarding the anticipated reactions of the firm's partners. Compensation systems cannot be imposed by management, but must be built from the ground up and take into account the firm's values and culture, along with the partners' views.

Fairness in Sharing of Profits

The primary goal of a partner compensation system is to fairly allocate the firm's profits among the partners. The goal seems simple enough, but measuring each partner's contribution can become hopeless if there is no consensus among the partners as to the relative importance of values brought to the firm. And beyond the issue of intrinsic fairness, the issue of perceived fairness looms. The compensation should do a relatively good job of rewarding each partner's contribution in the context of a process that is considered open, fair, and credible.

Compensation as a Management Tool

Compensation systems have evolved over the years. What was once simply considered a means to fairly compensating partners has now become a critical management tool. As law firms face greater financial challenges, law firm managers have begun to appreciate the fact that the compensation system is a tool that can drive the partners' actions. For example, if a compensation system rewards a certain behavior, then it is likely that the partners will engage in that behavior. On the other hand, if the compensation system does not reward a specific behavior, it will be unlikely that the partners will engage in that behavior. It can be the best tool for motivating individual partners' practices and performance.

A prime example of this problem is the firm with management reports that focus on the individual hours worked by partners, associates, and paralegals and the revenue produced by each person. It is not uncommon to see small firms reporting dollars beside the names of associates and paralegals. The signal being sent by management is that delegation by partners is not valued because the partner does not get dollar credit for the hours worked by the associate or the paralegal. In these firms, partners tend to hoard the work (so the dollars show up in their column) rather than delegating it to others. These firms do not give partners the incentive to focus on originating work and managing work performed by others, an essential strategy for any firm seeking to grow and prosper.

Another good example is the training and mentoring of associates. If the compensation system does not consider and reward lawyers for the training and mentoring of associates, then it is unlikely that the partners will be focused on that activity in any meaningful way. These are examples of management's need to create a compensation system that encourages partner behaviors that are in sync with the firm's goals and objectives.

Also, think of the compensation system as a living organism that may need to be modified occasionally. If the firm's needs change, it would be critical to utilize a compensation system that can be adjusted to encourage or discourage different behaviors. A change in the marketplace that results in a decline in the firm's business will signal a need to increase the reward for the origination of business. Similarly, an abundance of business will place greater value on those partners performing the services and delegating to others.

Other Partner Compensation Concepts

Before launching into a discussion of specific compensation systems, there are a number of general compensation concepts that should play into any consideration of making a change.

Money, Money, Money

This should come as no surprise:

> If revenue is short, no compensation system will work well.
> If revenue is good, almost any compensation system will work.

If the underlying problem is lack of revenue, don't assume that the problem can be solved by overhauling the compensation system. If the firm has a revenue problem, the solution should be finding ways to increase revenue. While tweaking the compensation system may be useful to provide different incentives, avoid the temptation to make wholesale changes to remedy a revenue shortage.

Healthy Tension

Also, accept the fact that the allocation of profits among the partners will cause tension. This tension can be healthy if the partners understand the workings of the compensation system and know how their actions will affect their compensation. Obviously, good communication and candid discussion are critical to managing the operation of the compensation system. Everyone's primary goal has to be focused on the firm's success as a whole and not the success of individuals.

An unhealthy compensation system is one that promotes internal competition among the partners whose energies should be directed externally. Internally competitive firms will lose in the marketplace.

Varied Contributions

It takes a mix of different talents and skills to serve clients. Differing skills may have differing values and will need to be rewarded based on the firm's relative value. Be forewarned that the firm with a compensation system focusing predominately on one skill will not emerge and attain its potential. In fact, many troubled firms are those that reward one skill to the exclusion of other skills.

"Raise All the Boats"

Most firms want a compensation system that will incentivize behaviors that will result in the firm as a whole doing well. The concept of *raising all the boats* means that if the firm does well, each individual will do well as a result. The reverse is not true. If certain individuals do well, that does not assure that the firm will do well.

Managing the Spread

In constructing and operating the partner compensation system, it is necessary to determine the spread between the highest compensated partners and the lowest compensated partners. The spread is individual to each firm and will depend on the firm's culture and the specific skills and abilities of the partners involved. While there is no survey data readily available on this point, a 3-to-1 ratio is relatively common. At the same time, a 2-to-1 ratio is not uncommon, nor is a 4-to-1 ratio. While these ranges may provide some guidance, the final decision has to be based on the uniqueness of the individual firm and the partners' relative contributions.

Retroactive versus Prospective

A retroactive compensation system provides a *drawer* during the year and then looks back at the end of the year to determine actual compensation and then a true-up. A prospective compensation system sets the compensation for next year based on the performance during the prior year or several years. The compensation or percentage share of profits is established at the start of the year.

The Five-Year Review

The firm's compensation system should be reviewed at least every five years. The purpose is twofold. First, existing partners may have forgotten how it is intended to work and new lawyers may have joined the partnership ranks without ever taking part in a comprehensive discussion of the compensation system. The review gets everyone back on the same page, which is a healthy place to be. Further, it may make sense to make adjustments to the system, even if relatively small, and those possible changes need airing and agreement. The compensation system needs to work well in a changing environment, so it should not be considered a static document.

Compensation Systems

There are four basic partner compensation systems that have been utilized by law firms. But within the four systems, there are variations which may include combining concepts from the different systems. Individual firms will tailor their system to meet their specific needs. It may be an exaggeration to say that there are no two firms with exactly the same system, but I have not seen two exactly alike.

Two compensation systems were developed in earlier times, but are rarely seen today. Equality, or the equal sharing of profits, is the traditional partnership concept. Some law firms adopted this traditional concept at inception, but found it difficult to maintain as the firm grew and the lawyers matured in their professional roles. The lock-step system is another compensation system that has lost favor in recent years. In this system, partners move up the compensation ladder in locked steps, on the basis that every partner at the same seniority level is of similar value. While equality and lock-step systems are rarely seen today, the majority of firms tend to utilize a formula system, a subjective system, or a combination of the two.

Equality System

An equal division of profits among partners seems logical when two or three lawyers of comparable experience establish a new firm. A lot can be said for the basic sharing concept of a true partnership. As time passes and new lawyers join the partnership ranks, however, the equality concept becomes more difficult to maintain.

Advantages	Disadvantages
Simple	Does not reward the superstar
Raises all the boats	No individual incentive to produce $$$
Rewards all types of efforts	Tends to carry unproductive partners

While the equality system has an idyllic appeal that satisfies our best side of human nature, it becomes difficult to maintain as partners progress in the profession to different levels or as newer, less experienced lawyers join the partnership ranks. With no individual incentive, there is a risk that the most competitive lawyers will leave and those who remain will tend toward a mediocre practice.

Lock-Step System

The lock-step system assumes that each lawyer will have relatively similar value as they progress through the seniority levels within the firm. The system involves several steps that enable a lawyer to move up the ladder from one step to the next, based solely on years with the firm.

Advantages	Disadvantages
Rewards seniority and loyalty	Fails to reward the superstar
Avoids fights about small differences	Provides no individual incentive
Rewards all types of efforts	Tends to carry unproductive partners
Focuses on the institution	

While the lock-step system has lost favor, there are components that have been incorporated into other systems. For example, the idea that allocating compensation is not a precise activity leads one to conclude that it makes no sense to try to draw fine distinctions. Can one really say that one person is worth $175,000 a year and another is worth $170,000? To avoid the impossible fine differences, some firms that have elected a subjective system have nevertheless utilized several levels (i.e., $125,000, $150,000, $175,000, and $200,000) and provide that the partners move from one step to the next based on subjective criteria. It is different from a true lockstep in that seniority is not the trigger for moving from one step to the next.

Formula System

Formula systems have been around for a long time and will continue into the future. Perhaps the most well-known formula system was that of Hale & Dorr, first publicized in the 1930s. Their original Hale & Dorr system was based on cash in the door and gave points in a formula for origination to the lawyer who brought the client in, hours worked, based on the lawyer who performed the services, and profitability to the lawyer who originated the work. The system also gave working-hour credit to the lawyers performing approved management functions. To provide stability, the system applied these points in the context of more than one year. Today, there are a number of firms that will say they are following a modified Hall & Dorr system.

Formula systems, sometimes referred to as *eat what you kill*, are fairly common in small firms where the lawyers are sharing the overhead, but choose to be compensated based on their own revenue performance.

Advantages	Disadvantages
Directly motivates individuals	Too much emphasis on getting clients and producing $$$
Direct correlation between revenue produced and compensation	Success comes to some individuals
Everyone understands the rules	Can result in disgruntled partners
	Results in weak management
	Ignores seniority
	Fails to serve the firm's long-range interests

A formula system can result in individual successes. In fact, in some cases every partner in a firm can be financially successful, but at a cost. That cost is likely to be weak management and a lack of succession planning, because it serves no one's individual interests to devote significant time to management and no one has the incentive to train and mentor the next generation of partners. There are examples of successful formula firms collapsing when the original generation of partners approaches retirement age. They joke about the last one having responsibility to shut off the lights.

Subjective System

Subjective compensation systems are the most common, particularly among mid-sized firms, with an institutional approach to the firm's success. A committee holding is usually responsible for recommending compensation in the form of points or percentages, based on a previously agreed to set of factors which may include financial performance as well as the more subjective contributions to the firm.

Subjective compensation systems, sometimes referred to as ***rough justice,*** involve a committee looking at billable hours, billings, receipts, and realization, etc., but not applying any math or formula to that data. The other difference from a formula type system is that the committee considers subjective factors like the partner's contributions to management, to the training and mentoring of associates, to teamwork, and to a whole variety of other ways the partner contributes to the overall success of the firm.

Advantages	Disadvantages
Considers non-monetary factors	May tend to support a seniority system
Rewards the team player	May under-compensate strong performers
Provides stability to the partners	Can result in favoritism
Concerned with the firm as an institution	
Promotes long-range strategic plans	

A subjective system allows for flexibility in planning. To position the firm for success in the future, it may be necessary to initiate a plan to develop a new practice area. Such a project might require a partner to devote a substantial amount of time and effort over a couple of years with no expected financial reward. With a subjective system, the firm can reward the partner for that type of effort in a circumstance where there will be no significant revenue in the short term.

Mixing and Matching Compensation Systems

After evaluating the basic compensation systems, law firms find aspects of differing systems useful and may end up incorporating parts of two or more systems. Here are several samples of firms that have mixed and matched compensation systems:

- The partners' respective *drawers* are set based on their respective contributions measured subjectively, but they share any additional compensation equally.
- Half of the anticipated compensation is based on a formula and the other half is established subjectively.
- The basic compensation is subjective and prospective, with a retrospectively applied bonus up to a certain dollar amount for any one or more partners who have an extraordinary year (meaning substantially exceeding expectations).
- The basic compensation is based on a formula, but with a bonus of up to a certain dollar amount for any one or more partners who have made a substantial non-monetary contribution to the firm's success.

Making Compensation Systems Work

Selecting or devising an appropriate partner compensation system is an important step, but equally important is the system's operation, which must be understood by all partners and considered fair. Each system is vulnerable to failure in application, so constant vigilance is necessary.

- *Be sensitive to any perceived unfairness.* The firm leaders and managers need to be attentive to any concern that the system is or may be becoming unfair. It may be important to have a culture that allows for open and candid discussions of the issue. In fact, a discussion at an annual retreat would provide an ideal forum.
- *Maintain good financial records.* The partners need to have continued confidence that sharing profits equally is fair. To make that judgment, be sure to have a good set of monthly financial reports that reflect each aspect of financial performance.
- *Have accurate data.* A subjective system involves the general consideration of the financial performance of each partner. In order to make those subjective judgments, it is necessary to have complete and accurate information. Trouble abounds if there is a sense that the data circulated in unreliable.

- ***Consider sharing firm management burdens.*** Provide for each partner to participate in some aspect of non-billable functions so that there will be a fair division of those responsibilities.
- ***Make sure every partner understands the system.*** While this advice seems obvious, there are reported instances where the formula was so complicated that some partners did not understand how compensation was calculated.
- ***Make sure the factors to be considered are understood.*** Don't let the process be a mystery because one of more of the partners may not know what factors the committee is considering. The process needs to be completely transparent.
- ***Follow an agreed to and published process.*** Subjective systems work best when there is a high level of trust among the partners. The partners need to know who decides on compensation and the exact process involved to reach the result.

Professional Legal Staff 10

For large and small firms alike, making wise professional staffing decisions can profoundly affect the firm's productivity and its profitability. The legal staff can be made up of lawyers and paralegals who work on substantive matters in support of the partners and clients of the firm. In developing the professional staff, partners are no longer limited to the hiring of partner-track associates. An increasing number of lawyers are looking for nontraditional employment arrangements and paralegals are continuing to take on an increasing portion of the substantive legal work under a lawyer's supervision.

Growing a Strong Firm

Today's associates are tomorrow's partners, and represent the firm's future. Law firm managers should never underestimate the importance of hiring and developing associates as part of the firm's growth strategy and its need for succession planning. At the same time, firms must be careful not to aggressively recruit partner-track associates simply to satisfy current workload demands. Growing the firm with partner-track associates and adding workers to perform needed services should be treated as two separate but related issues.

Managing partners and administrators have come to realize the importance of avoiding the creation of a partner-heavy firm, a problem caused by aggressive hiring and liberal partnership policies in the 1970s and 1980s. A financially healthy firm has the optimum number of partners based on the community, the legal marketplace, and the firm's client base. If the current need is for manpower to perform work, consider the following possibilities:

Paralegals

The paralegal profession has developed rapidly over the past thirty years, based on the fact that a substantial portion of client work does not fit within the narrow definition of the *practice of law*. While paralegals are not allowed to accept cases and set fees for the firm, give legal advice to clients, plan strategy, negotiate with adversaries, appear in court or take depositions, they can perform most other work in a law office so long as it is done under the supervision of a lawyer who has ultimate responsibility for the work. Much of the work that associates are hired for could be performed by paralegals. Associate hiring decisions should not be made in a vacuum, but rather in conjunction with paralegal hiring decisions. The question to be addressed is whether the firm needs the help of a paralegal or an associate and it should be based on the nature of the work that needs to be covered.

Legal Assistants

In the early years of the paralegal profession, the titles of paralegal and legal assistant were used interchangeably for non-lawyers who performed substantive services under a lawyer's supervision. There were a few firms that used both terms and defined them differently, but even in those firms there was no consistency of approach. During the 1990s, the National Association of Legal Secretaries changed its name to the National Association of Legal Professionals and eliminated the title of secretary and began promoting their members as Lawyer's Assistants. As that change began to be implemented in law firms across the country, the confusion about titles increased. As a result, the paralegal profession is now promoting the title of paralegal, and the title legal assistant is largely being abandoned by the profession.

Freelance Paralegals

In addition to traditional paralegal positions within the law firm, most communities have freelance paralegals who are available for work on defined projects and support firms' needs for temporary help.

Permanent Associates

Each succeeding generation of lawyers brings a different culture to the law firm. New lawyers who have joined firms in recent years have a greater focus on balance and lifestyle. Many are content to take advantage of the relatively high salaries paid to associates who are content working in positions that do not offer partnership opportunities.

Contract Lawyers

Some firms have large projects that do not justify hiring a permanent associate and, as a result, those firms began hiring contract lawyers with a term of employment limited by the duration of the project.

Of Counsel

One of the most frequently asked questions is: *What does Of Counsel mean?* And each time the question is asked, the answer is different and, in some respect, unsatisfactory. Perhaps the best response is that an *Of Counsel* is a non-partner lawyer who has a contractual relationship with the firm, but holds a certain status based on age or past performance that makes it inappropriate to use the title permanent associate or contract lawyer. It is often used for laterals of partner-level status or senior lawyers preparing to transition into retirement.

While work can be performed by lawyers or paralegals who have no potential for partnership, firms need to address the bigger picture concerning the firm's growth and succession planning. Once a decision is made as to the partnership's desired growth, the firm will need to hire partner-track associates to foster the need for measured growth and be in a position to groom them as successors of the firm's current leaders.

Hiring Associates versus Hiring Paralegals

For the small law firm, no decision is more difficult or risky than when to hire an associate. A good decision can grow the firm and position it to provide better service to clients and more profits to the partners. A bad decision can undermine the financial health of the firm and its future. Mid-sized firms may have more experience with hiring decisions but, unless they have been both astute and lucky, these decisions can be risky. And for the largest firms, often the question is how many to hire and the mix between associates and paralegals. Firms of all sizes can face difficulties as a result of bad decisions.

Regardless of the firm's size, you will want to consider three separate aspects of the situation in making a decision. First, you will want to assess the circumstances of the firm's need. For example, if the need is to hire someone to meet with new clients, give legal advice, take depositions, or handle court hearings or trials, your need is clearly for a lawyer. On the other hand, if your need is for someone to be in more of a supportive role, investigating matters, collecting information, interviewing witnesses, preparing drafts of documents or pleadings, etc., then it may be wise to hire a qualified paralegal rather than an associate. In considering that analysis, it is important to recognize that talents and skills of lawyers and paralegals are different. Lawyers tend to focus on the law, strategy, and the big picture. Paralegals tend to be better organized, more thorough in their work, better on detail, follow-up, client communication and providing empathy.

The next step is to evaluate the impact that hiring an associate or a paralegal will have on the firm's profits. While complex formulas are available in other publications, the *Rule of Three* is an excellent starting point for a profitability analysis. Under the *Rule of Three,* the firm wants the associate or paralegal to be responsible for revenues that are three times the person's salary. The first third goes to salary. The second third is attributed to benefits and overhead, while the final third is considered profit.

Based on hourly rates ranging between $60 and $175, the chart below demonstrates how this test can be applied.

Hourly Rate	x	Billable Hours	=	Revenue	div by 3	=	Salary
$175		1,800		$315,000			$105,000
$150		1,600		$240,000			$ 80,000
$125		1,500		$187,500			$ 62,500
$100		1,500		$150,000			$ 50,000
$ 75		1,500		$112,500			$ 37,500
$ 60		1,500		$ 90,000			$ 30,000

Have in mind that the number of billable hours is a variable that will affect the analysis, as will the hourly rate charged for the associate or paralegal time. While the chart reflects hourly rates and billable hours found in many small and mid-sized firms, it may not include rates or hours commensurate with large, urban law firms.

The final aspect of the analysis involves the desired growth of the firm. Associates may become partners and share in the profits of the firm. In return for a few years of producing profits, the associates may be elevated to a position entitling them to a lifetime of sharing profits. Paralegals can provide profits for their entire career and will never share them with you as partners.

Think about an approach to associate hiring that focuses mostly on the desired growth of the partnership ranks and an approach to paralegal hiring that focuses on supporting the partners' work and returning longevity of profits to the firm.

Training and Mentoring Associates

Experience tells us that about one out of ten associates will be successful, regardless of whether they have some form of training or mentoring. It doesn't take long to pick out the superstars. But what about the others? Their success will depend in large part on the training, guidance, and mentoring they receive when they start their careers.

It is reported that associates desire training more than money. More associates become disenchanted with law firms because of the lack of training than any other reason. The associate is looking for help and guidance to create a career.

As the legal profession has become more competitive, most lawyers have found it necessary to work longer hours. As a result, the profession-wide trend is away from committing the time and energy to training associates. At the same time, there is less opportunity for new lawyers to "carry the partner's bag" and to gain meaningful experiences, due to client imposed restrictions.

Mentoring continues to get lip service, but most lawyers find it nearly impossible to accomplish, even with good intentions. Inadequate associate training can result in poor performance, client dissatisfaction, excessive write-offs, low morale, costly turnover, and partner dissatisfaction.

Every firm that recruits entry-level associates should have a program that provides orientation, training, evaluations, mentoring, and career planning.

Orientation

An orientation program should include a tour of the office, introductions to the managing partner and administrative staff, training on office systems, a review of office policies, and an understanding of the critical practice management and law office management concepts. Depending on the size of the firm and the complexity of the issues, the orientation can take place in one day or for a few hours a day over the course of the first week or two.

Training

There was a time when training programs involved rotating associates through several practice groups to provide the associate with a good foundation in several of the basic practice areas. While that goal is commendable, many firms have given up broad training and instead focus associates on the work of one practice group to make them profitable more quickly. Regardless of the breadth of training, an associate training program should include the substantive aspects of their practice area, client dynamics, public speaking and communication skills, legal writing, intake and billing practices, case planning, and practice management.

Evaluations

The evaluation of associates can be formal or informal. The best training includes timely feedback from the partner on each matter. Unfortunately, partners are not good at critiquing work as matters proceed, even in the circumstance where the associate welcomes it. The next best approach is to conduct formal evaluations on an annual or semi-annual basis. The evaluation process will include utilization of a standard form to obtain input from the partners who work with the associate, a synthesis of the input, the creation of a message for the associate, as to areas of concern and goals for improvement, and a salary adjustment that can be conducted in connection with the evaluation, or separately at a different time.

Mentoring

The best mentoring is a natural process. A partner and associate develop a working relationship and the partner becomes a mentor, without the need for an assignment or a structure. These natural associations work best. Efforts to establish and implement mentoring plans with specific assignments commonly fail. For formal structured mentoring to stand a chance of working, the partners need to have bought in to the program and appreciate its importance to the future of the firm.

Career Planning

High on the list of associate concerns is career planning. Will the time spent with the firm advance the associate's career? Is the firm concerned about helping the associate develop a career? Or, is the firm only focused on the short-term profits the associate can produce? Because of the importance of career planning to the associate, firms that include this career planning as part of their associate evaluation program will have a better chance of retaining their best associates.

While the law firm needs to have a structure in place for associate training, the associate needs to understand that they share in the responsibility for their own development. Lawyers charged with recruiting new associates need to explore the candidates' attitudes and expectations in order to attract and acquire lawyers who are focused on their careers and recognize that their development is a shared responsibility.

Understanding the Paralegal Advantage

The paralegal profession has revolutionized the practice of law. While we can make a list of the many advantages paralegals provide, the true benefit is based on the fact that when paralegals are properly integrated in the delivery of legal services, lawyers can raise the practice of law to its highest level.

Properly trained and supervised, paralegals provide solid value to clients. They make significant contributions that advance the client's objectives and are normally more appreciated by the clients as the favored contact for routine communications. As lawyers have been able to expand the role of paralegals, they have lowered the overall cost to the client, while improving their own profits.

The goal of most paralegal programs is to expand the role to the extent possible, based on the Rules of Professional Conduct and depending on the skills and talents of the individual paralegals. In thinking about the paralegal role, consider the ABA's original definition of paralegals which defined their role, by stating in part:

> . . . which involves the performance, under the ultimate direction and supervision of a lawyer, of specifically delegated substantive legal work, which work, for the most part, requires sufficient knowledge of legal concepts that, absence such assistant, the lawyer would perform the task.

Paralegals need to steer clear of those functions that define the practice of law, which have been generally described as follows:

- Setting fees and accepting cases
- Providing legal advice
- Planning strategy and the course of a case
- Taking depositions
- Negotiating with adversaries
- Handling court hearings and trials

Most other work in advancing the client's case or matter is not considered the *practice of law* and is proper work for paralegals, if performed under the supervision of a lawyer.

Contributing to Law Firm Profits

Paralegals can produce significant profits for lawyers, if their work is properly managed and adequately priced. However, before launching into a financial analysis, it is important to understand that some benefits are difficult to reduce to a mathematical formula. Let's start by evaluating the elements of a paralegal's contribution to the firm.

- Revenues from paralegal hours
- An increase in the lawyer's hourly rate that is justified by shifting a larger portion of the routine work to a paralegal, leaving more complex and sophisticated work for the lawyer

- The increase in the number of billable hours that results from moving non-billable work from the lawyer to the paralegal (although the best result would be to move the non-billable work to other staff)
- The improved quality of life, personally and professionally, for the lawyer who has the confidence that the paralegal has matters properly organized and under control

Some of these benefits cannot be easily defined. For instance, how does one assess the benefit of having a paralegal perform less productive work, so the lawyer can be more productive, attending to the more challenging aspects of the law practice? Similarly, how does one quantify the benefit of having the paralegal relieve the lawyer of non-billable practice management functions? Although these factors may be important and must be considered, they should be carefully analyzed to determine whether they are providing a significant benefit rather than an excuse to maintain an unprofitable practice or on unprofitable paralegal. Remember, a paralegal is an income producer; in most cases, billable work should be a priority.

However, the goal is to develop or recruit career paralegals that will remain with the firm long term. In most circumstances, the lawyer can justify billing an experienced paralegal at double the rate of an entry-level paralegal. Even if the firm pays an experienced paralegal twice as much as the entry-level paralegal, under normal circumstances the profits generated by the experienced paralegal can be greater. It is the overhead costs that make this so. They will be nearly the same for both paralegals.

Consider the following:

	Entry-level	Experienced
Salary	$40,000	$ 80,000
Fringe Benefits and Overhead Costs	$35,000	$ 40,000
Total Costs	$75,000	$120,000
Hours	1,500	1,500
Hourly Rate	x 60	x 120
Potential Revenues	$90,000	$180,000
Less 10 % Uncollectible	$ 9,000	$ 18,000
	$81,000	$162,000
Less Costs	$75,000	$120,000
Profit	$ 6,000	$ 42,000

Modifications can be made to the model based on individual circumstances, but the important point from a profitability standpoint is setting the goal of developing and retaining experienced paralegals.

Shifting Work to Paralegals Will Justify Higher Lawyer Hourly Rates

Lawyers have been overqualified for many tasks they have performed in the past. To the extent that well-qualified paralegals can take on a larger portion of the work, the lawyer can justify a higher hourly rate for a more limited role, without increasing the cost to the client. Consider the following:

Lawyer Intensive Staffing

40 lawyer hours at $200	=	$8,000
16 paralegal hours at $90	=	$1,400
56 Hours	Amount of Bill	$9,400

Now, assume the lawyer learns how to expand the role of the paralegal and is able to shift a substantial portion of the work.

Paralegal Intensive Staffing

16 lawyer hours at $250	=	$4,000
48 paralegal hours at $90	=	$4,320
64 Hours	Amount of Bill	$8,320

In the second example, it is assumed the work shifted to the paralegal will take more time than if it had been performed by the lawyer. Even so, note that the lawyer's hourly rate can be increased to $250 and yet the client has a lower cost. Who could ask for more?

In justifying an hourly rate of $250 instead of $200, the lawyer can produce significant additional revenue.

1,500 hours x $250	=	$375,000
1,500 hours at $200	=	$300,000
Increased billings		$75,000
Lost 10% for uncollectibles		$7,500
Increased revenues per lawyer		$67,500

The lawyer also is able to handle a larger volume of legal work. A lawyer who dedicates an average of forty hours to each file can handle thirty-seven files a year. A lawyer who dedicates an average of sixteen hours to each file can handle ninety-three files a year.

The concept is significant. By shifting a larger portion of the work to paralegals, the lawyer is able to handle an increased volume of legal work at a higher hourly rate. The ability to increase the amount of legal work per lawyer will be a significant advantage in the years ahead.

Let's carry this example through to its conclusion. If the lawyer is producing a profit on the work of three paralegals and is increasing his or her revenues from a higher hourly rate, the net gain may look something like this:

Profit on paralegal #1	$ 42,000
Profit on paralegal #2	$ 42,000
Profit on paralegal #3	$ 42,000
	$126,000
Increased profits from higher lawyer hourly rates	$ 67,500
Total additional profits generated by shifting work to three paralegals	$193,500

Is it as easy as it sounds? Probably not. Will you be able to implement this change next Monday morning? No. But if you work at applying these concepts you should be able to increase your profits over time by adding paralegals, and shifting billable work to them, and gradually increasing your hourly rates.

A common mistake is not setting billable hour requirements for paralegals. Keep in mind that most paralegals have no responsibility for client development, community involvement, or firm management. Their primary role is to produce work-billable hours. While the paralegal billable hour requirement should not be as high as the associates' requirement, it should not be far behind.

To the extent paralegals meet or exceed their billable hour requirements, they may be returning significant profits to the firm. As a result, some firms have developed bonus programs to reward paralegals who produce high totals of hours. The greater the number of hours worked by the paralegal and billed by the firm, the greater the profits.

Key Ingredients for Success

Some firms have had enormous success in the utilization of paralegals. Some have achieved only modest success, while others have failed miserably. By taking a look at the firms with the most successful paralegal programs, the following key ingredients are always present.

The Lawyer and Client Have Confidence in the Paralegal

Confidence makes all the difference. If the lawyer has confidence in the paralegal, all things are possible. The clients will take their cue from the lawyer. If the lawyer lacks confidence in the paralegal, the clients will take notice and act accordingly.

The firm should look for individuals with good analytical abilities, good writing and oral communication skills, maturity, judgment, common sense, initiative, dedication, a professional attitude, and willingness to learn and expand their skills.

The other aspect of developing confidence involves selecting a paralegal who is a good match with the lawyer. Some lawyers have difficult personalities. Some have large egos (slight understatement). When putting together a lawyer-paralegal team, some combinations work better than others. Finding the correct personalities to work together is not always easy but, in the last analysis, chemistry will have a large affect on whether the lawyer and paralegal are able to develop a successful working relationship.

Assign the Proper Work and Expand the Role

Many paralegals serve in limited roles because their supervising lawyers do not understand the applicable ethical restraints. As contrary as it may sound, an understanding of those limits is important to expanding the role. Any lawyer who is uncertain about the ethical limitations will be reluctant to expand the role.

Rule 5.5 of the Rules of Professional Conduct provides that non-lawyers cannot do those things that amount to the "practice of law." The difficult issue, of course, becomes what is the definition of the practice of law. While lawyers must be guided by local rules, it is generally accepted that paralegals cannot:

- Accept cases
- Set fees
- Give legal advice
- Plan strategy
- Negotiate with adversaries
- Make legal decisions
- Appear in court

Under the supervision of a lawyer, paralegals can perform most other tasks. The lawyer needs to be well versed in these rules before they can effectively expand the paralegal role. In the 1990s, the American Bar Association adopted a definition of paralegal work which ended with the words:

"... absent [the paralegal] the lawyer would perform the task"

The definition is telling us that the work should not be clerical, but rather work that has been traditionally performed by lawyers. Courts have adopted that definition in deciding whether paralegal time can be charged in fee-shifting cases.

The Paralegal Has Full Involvement on the Files

If paralegals are expected to perform "lawyer work," they must have involvement on the files, much like the lawyers who otherwise would have performed the tasks. The paralegals need to establish a rapport with clients, understand the issues of the case, understand the client's objective, and be generally informed of what is going on at all times. Only with a complete understanding of these matters can the paralegal effectively take on this high level of responsibility.

The Lawyer Properly Prices the Paralegal's Work

Properly managed and properly priced, paralegal work can generate significant profits. However, it takes a careful financial analysis of the paralegal work to assure profits are being achieved.

Practice Groups 11

Practice groups bring lawyers, paralegals, and staff together to coordinate practice management and facilitate the delivery of quality legal services. These groups can be organized according to areas of the law, a specific industry or client, or a type of service. The breakdown that works for one firm may not apply to another. Each firm needs to examine its client base and practice areas and come up with a customized structure that works for managing its lawyers in the delivery of legal services.

Large firms may have departments, which can provide an umbrella for several smaller practice groups. For example, the firm may have a Litigation Department, made up of a Commercial Litigation Practice Group, a White-Collar Crime Practice Group and a Personal Injury Practice Group.

As the firm's management process evolves, practice group leaders often take on additional responsibilities and participate with firm management by providing input on the revenue budget, evaluating the need for resources, monitoring the productivity and profitability of practice group members, and assisting with the evaluations of partners, associates, paralegals, and staff.

Practice Group Organization

A practice group should have an effective leader, a vice chair or secretary, a clearly defined outline of responsibilities, and a regular meeting schedule. The structure should also include some basis of integration with firm management and the work of the firm's administrator.

Leadership

Who do we want for practice group chair? The best way to start this discussion is to understand who should not be chair. The firm's strongest rainmaker should not be chair. The group's most senior lawyer should not be chair, nor its most productive lawyer. Also, be sure to avoid the lawyer with poor client skills or inefficient practice methods. The number of acceptable candidates may be small.

The best choice may be the mid-level partner who has exhibited both good practice management skills and leadership potential. Often, the position of practice group chair is a proving ground for individuals to demonstrate their leadership abilities and their potential as future leaders of the firm.

Practice Group Members

There are several different approaches to practice groups. Some firms may limit involvement to that of lawyers and paralegals. A more inclusive approach is to include lawyers, paralegals, and all staff that work within the practice group. Some firms hold two meetings a month, one limited to partners and the other to include associates, paralegals, and staff. In the last analysis, the level of inclusion should depend on who is needed at the meetings to achieve the group's goals.

Meetings

Practice group meetings should be informational, educational, and project driven. The meeting agenda should be well organized and the leader must guide the group though the topics in an effective and concise manner.

Let's face it. Some lawyers cannot run a good meeting. If the chair lacks that skill, control will be lost, meetings will go on endlessly, and the attendees will consider it a waste of time, thereby affecting future attendance. Training your practice group chairs how to run an effective meeting might be time and money well spent.

The Delivery of Services

A practice group's primary function is to manage the delivery of services by encouraging or requiring lawyers to coordinate their efforts, comply with agreed-to policies, and develop useful resources. The practice group's charge may include:

- ■ *Encouraging specialization.* The practice group should encourage lawyers to narrow their practices and coordinate with other lawyers to avoid unnecessary duplication and assure that the firm has lawyers with experience in each aspect of a practice area.

- *Promoting teamwork.* The chair should keep the group focused on what is best for the client being served and the firm as a whole. This may involve encouraging team work where appropriate and in some circumstances, shifting work from one lawyer to another.
- *Developing resources.* Practice groups should have responsibility for creating and updating forms, maintaining a work product retrieval system, developing unified systems for the performance of basic segments of the client service, identifying needed resources, and making staffing recommendations. They should also have responsibility for technology needs.
- *Establishing policies.* Practice groups are the place for adopting policies that apply to its specific practice areas, including client intake, standardized fee deposits, fee methods and pricing, as well as quality control and client service standards.
- *Continuing legal education.* Practice groups have responsibility for monitoring and/or recommending CLE for its members, including its partners, associates, and paralegals. In some firms, the practice group has ultimate responsibility for deciding how its share of the CLE budget will be disbursed.

Practice groups are also the forum for orchestrating a sharing of CLE information, perhaps through reporting at its meetings of pertinent CLE sessions attended by its members.

- *Training of associates and paralegals.* Practice groups have responsibility for creating and conducting training sessions for its associates and paralegals.
- *Evaluating associates and paralegals.* The practice group chair, along with the partners in the group, should have a primary role and significant input into the evaluations and salary adjustments for its associates and paralegals.
- *Reviewing new files.* A review of new files at practice group meetings serves several useful purposes. Lawyers and paralegals become aware of files involving similar issues and they are able to benefit from the sharing of information and resources. There is always a benefit to lawyers better understanding each other's practices. And by being informed of all significant cases handled by the lawyers in the practice group, lawyers are informed of subtle conflicts not exposed by electronic methods of checking.
- *Recognizing emerging issues.* The practice group provides a forum for discussion of emerging issues which if investigated early can put the firm in a favorable competitive advantage.
- *Planning marketing.* Practice groups are in the best position to develop and implement its own marketing plan.

Once the plan is approved by firm management, a member of the practice group should be assigned responsibility for monitoring the implementation of the plan.

Productivity and Revenue Issues

One of the most difficult issues facing law firm management is developing a realistic revenue budget each year. Unlike the expense side, management has no control over the factors that result in revenue coming in the door. As law firms grow and mature, they realize it is the practice group, which is one step closer to the action, that is in a better spot to predict and manage both productivity and the resulting cash flow. Revenue is a direct result of adequate in-take policies, good practice management, strong client service, and appropriately set legal fee arrangements.

Productivity

Productivity standards are essential to a well-run firm, whether measured by hours, monthly billings realization, receipts, or a combination of those factors. Shortfalls in expected revenue can result from any number of factors, including poor time recording, ineffective time management, inefficiencies in the delivery of services, laziness, and/or lack of work. Assessing the particular reasons with regard to any individual is best conducted by the practice group leader, who will have responsibility for assisting lawyers with their practice methods and shifting of work when some lawyers have too much work, while others have too little.

Revenue Accountability

Practice group leaders are well positioned to assist firm management in creating a revenue budget by analyzing past performance of the group's lawyers and providing guidance and support to the lawyers charged with increasing productivity. Once the revenue budget is set and allocated among the practice groups, each of the practice group leaders should review performance on a monthly basis, keeping the lawyers in their practice group informed of both the group's progress and individual's progress. The practice group leader should keep management advised of any adjustments to the group's revenue projections.

The practice group leader will need to keep productivity and revenue accountability on the agenda for practice group meetings. In addition, the leader may need to counsel with lawyers individually to address shortfalls and assist in devising a remedy.

Integration with Firm Management

There are several approaches to integrating practice group chairs into firm management. Some firms have management committees made up of practice group chairs. Other firms have practice group chairs report to firm management, whether a managing partner or a management committee. There are no right or wrong answers. The best approach is to determine what works best for the firm, based on management structure and cultural factors at play.

Succession Planning 12

A law firm's continued existence depends on a well-planned transition from one generation to the next. Most large firms operate with well-designed succession planning, without which they never would have survived. Unfortunately, many small and mid-sized firms get into serious trouble by ignoring the need for succession planning, which leads to an unexpected crisis when the founder or current leader announces plans to retire without anyone prepared to take over. The problem of transition is exacerbated by the tendency of most senior lawyers to keep their thoughts about retirement to themselves until the last minute, as they fear any early disclosure would put them at risk for reduced compensation or a decline in clout within the firm.

While succession planning problems tend to be most acute in smaller firms, issues resulting from lack of planning can plague a firm of any size.

The Transition Crisis

Ironically, the longer a strong leader has been in charge of a successful firm, the bigger the problem. The firm's success will lull partners into a sense of security, causing them not to worry about leadership issues or the need to groom a successor. Perhaps there is a bit of denial at play. Then, the unthinkable happens. The firm's leader announces retirement plans or, even worse, becomes disabled or gets hit by a bus and dies. It is only then that the other partners take stock of the contributions to the firm that need to be replaced, which will likely involve leadership, management, and client origination.

Owners of small firms rarely focus on developing successors. Typically, they hire lawyers to work cases, serve the firm's clients, and return a profit to the firm's owners. With no attention to career planning or grooming associates for partnership, turnover is commonplace. The associates who do remain on the job tend to be those lawyers who have no entrepreneurial spirit and no desire or ability to accept ownership responsibilities. When the owner suddenly recognizes the need to groom a successor, there are no acceptable candidates that have remained with the firm.

In many small firms, the awakening comes too late. Some firms scramble to find an affiliation at the last minute; others end up turning off the lights. It doesn't have to be that way.

When to Address Succession Planning

Succession planning needs to occur when the current leaders of the firm are in their forties or early fifties. It takes a minimum of ten years to develop successors.

The message to law firm leaders is clear: Bite the bullet! You are not going to live forever. And even if you do, you are not going to want to practice law forever. Trust me. Think about the benefits of having supportive partners in the wings prepared to pick up the load when you reach the age when your energy declines or, more importantly, when you suddenly realize there is more to life than working.

The responsibility of raising attention to the issue and developing a plan rests with the firm's leader, not the younger lawyers who may consider raising the issue political suicide. Like most good ideas, there will be risk involved. Choose your successors carefully. Be prepared to support and mentor them and hope for the best.

Partnership Track

The firm's recruitment effort needs to include the fact that the firm offers partnership opportunities to attract lawyers committed to the profession and their future. The opportunity for partnership is at the foundation of any succession-planning strategy.

Applicants being recruited should be told about the opportunities, the criteria, the process, and the timeline. A guarantee of partnership is not necessary or desirable, but there is a need for a clear statement of both the opportunities and the rules that apply.

Ownership Training

It is relatively easy to distinguish the associates with an employee mentality from those with an ownership mentality. With some, this distinction finds its roots in an individual's personality traits. With most, however, it is a developed condition based on the associate's training experiences within the firm.

All associates should be exposed to what it takes to be an owner or a leader of the law firm. Some law schools offer elective courses in law practice management and students who have taken those courses graduate several steps ahead of the colleagues. Unfortunately, the vast majority of law students graduate without the benefit of any such course. Therefore, once in the law firm, every opportunity should be taken to expose associates to the firm's management workings.

Associate training programs should include annual associate evaluations which specifically address whether the associate is developing the knowledge and the skill necessary to be considered for partnership.

Transitioning Clients

Let's start with a warning. Don't live with a false sense of security concerning the firm's ability to retain clients following a senior partner's departure. As tight as a client/partner relationship may be, that loyalty may not translate to the firm as a whole. For example, the successful business client will have developed many lawyer contacts, but never be tempted to switch lawyers. With a lawyer's retirement, however, the client is likely to use the opportunity to connect with and engage one of his or her other lawyer acquaintances. Under those circumstances, retaining the client within the retiring lawyer's firm is a greater challenge than most lawyers appreciate.

A succession plan needs to include a long-term effort to expose important clients to a number of lawyers within the firm. That effort will increase the likelihood that clients will consider the firm as their legal counsel, not just one individual. The process will have to be carried out with finesse, so as to not undercut the client's ties to the senior lawyer.

Transitioning Leadership

A leadership transition within a law firm should be seamless and according to a plan previously developed by the partners. Controversy at the time of transition should be avoided at all costs. Any change in a management committee should be in accordance with an ongoing process. In a managing partner model, the successor should be identified early and groomed for the position, perhaps serving as an assistant for several years.

Sometimes, the best approach in replacing the founder/managing partner is to evolve to a management committee model with three members, with staggered three-year terms. With that approach, it is common to have the retiring founder/managing partner serve on the committee for the first year, and then rotate off the committee. That provides both continuity and an opportunity for the new members of the management team to learn from the retiring founder/managing partner.

Grooming lawyers for future management roles is an ongoing process. All partners should be considered and efforts should be made to assess their potential as future leaders of the firm. This may involve assessing their role as practice group leaders or as the chair of other committees. The process will narrow the acceptable candidates to a precious few. A significant percentage of lawyers simply do not have the necessary skills to serve in a leadership role and, unfortunately, some of the few lawyers who seek the role may not be the best choice.

Incentivizing the Senior Lawyer

A successful succession plan will always protect the senior lawyer who is being asked to give up a portion of client control and become expendable by grooming a successor. This brings us back to the use of the all-important compensation process which rewards any behavior we want to encourage. Under some existing formula compensation systems, the sharing of clients with others may lead to a reduction in compensation. For a client transition plan to work, the compensation issue must offer a level of protection to any partner being asked to start the transition process of moving clients to other lawyers.

If the firm has funded a defined contribution plan or a defined benefit plan, the senior partner may have financial security built into the program. But, if there is no firm retirement plan, then the senior lawyer may feel compelled to hang onto the control of clients as a means of maintaining his or her share of the income flow. Any effort to create a succession plan requires a close look at both the compensation system and the existing retirement benefits provided by the firm.

The Role of Senior Lawyers

Senior lawyers in a wind-down mode are an untapped resource in many firms. Senior partners who remain active in the community continue to develop contacts and broaden their range of acquaintances. These lawyers should be encouraged to support new leadership, mentor younger lawyers, and focus on marketing the firm and its younger lawyers.

Once again, the compensation system looms as a critical factor in getting senior lawyers to shift their focus from hanging on to client work to mentoring, marketing, and promoting the firm in the community.

A Step-By-Step Guide to Better Goverance

Law firms must enact necessary changes to their governance process if they are to have the best chances at surviving and thriving. Unfortunately, many lawyers are set in their ways and resist change, even in circumstances where their firm's survival may be at stake. To overcome this resistance, leadership needs to be armed with a methodical, well-founded plan and compelling reasons for initiating the needed change.

It is imperative that due diligence be performed and that changes are not blindly offered up. Partners will end up taking opposite sides of the issue and once that happens, the chance of consensus is gone. Lawyers are take-charge people, skilled at getting their way. Once they have taken a position on an issue, they likely will not admit they have been wrong. The adversarial nature of their profession finds its way to the partnership table. As a result, law firm leaders have to persuade lawyers one by one of the need for change before allowing them to take a position at a partnership meeting. Get your votes lined up in advance.

To assist in implementing changes to governance addressed in Part II, Part III provides practical, step-by-step procedures with regard to each of the governance topics. The Appendices provide the sample forms, policies, and worksheets necessary to implement each recommendation. Be thorough, be prepared, and find the votes!

Strengthening the Partnership 13

If the firm has no written agreement, make it a priority. Take the time to conduct a comprehensive review of all potential partnership issues and consider amending, or in some cases, creating your partnership agreement. Better governance starts with a complete partnership agreement.

How tragic if the firm implodes, or ends up in litigation, because the partners did not care enough or did not make it a priority to document their agreement. And even if there is an agreement, it may not be adequate as an effective governing document which effectively covers the inherent risks of a law partnership.

Step 1: Evaluate the Terms of the Partnership Agreement

What would happen in your present firm if one of your partners became disabled, died, or decided to withdraw and set up a practice across the street? Does your partnership agreement adequately spell out the partners' rights and duties under the circumstances? Or, would there be unanswered questions leading to controversy or something worse?

Lawyers tend to live with the status quo and do nothing so long as they are not faced with crisis. However, they should not be lulled into a sense of false security because nothing bad has happened. It takes only one issue arising at an inopportune moment to put a firm at great risk. The discussion that follows will raise a number of issues that require attention in the partnership agreement.

Partners

The agreement should identify the partners and provide the criteria and process for adding new partners to the ranks. How is that decision going to be made? What is required in terms of a vote? Is a simple majority sufficient or should the admission of new partners require a supermajority? Should there be a buy-in and, if so, how is the amount calculated?

Most firms believe that the admission of partners is one of the most significant decisions to be made and new partners should not be added on a close vote. As a result, firms typically require a supermajority vote, which could be a two-thirds or a three-quarters vote or, in small firms, perhaps a unanimous vote.

The next question is: Should there be a buy-in requirement? If so, in what amount? Smaller firms tend to require new partners to pay for their interest in the firm. The buy-in can provide additional capital for the firm or can be used to compensate the existing partners for their investment and sweat equity in creating the law firm or in growing it in size. The best approach in setting the amount is to include a formula in the partnership agreement for determining the firm's value, to which the new partner's percentage interest can be applied. Most firms allow for a buy-in over several years or, alternatively, the firm directs the new partner to a friendly bank, with the firm co-signing the note. Firms that do have a buy-in provision also typically provide for a payment to partners upon departure.

In recent years, there has been an increasing number of large firms that have adopted a free buy-in. Under that approach, there are no payments to departing partners. That is referred to as *free in, free out.*

Obviously, the partnership agreement will need to specify whether there is a single tier of partners or two tiers of partners. If the firm has two tiers of partners, it will be necessary for the agreement to specify the differences in their rights and duties. The second-tier partners will likely have a different ownership interest in the firm, different voting rights, and a different compensation arrangement. Second-tier partners are not normally required to buy in and are not responsible for the firm's debts.

Another area of partnership concern is the topic of outside activities. Typically, the partnership agreement provides that all monies earned from the practice of law are to be paid to the partnership. There are a number of income opportunities related to the law which would not come under a strict definition of the practice of law; for example, should payments received from teaching a law school class in the evening be treated as revenue to the law firm? How about royalties from a book on governing law firms? How about monies received from serving on a board of directors? Or holding political office? These questions should be addressed in advance.

Duration

The Uniform Partnership Act controls issues not specifically addressed in the partnership agreement. That would mean that unless the duration of the partnership is addressed, the death of one of the partners would terminate the partnership. As a result, most law firm partnership agreements have a provision that the partnership will survive a partner's death. This provision is not necessary in a professional association or a limited liability company (LLC).

Capital

Law firms require capital to fund startup, to survive irregular cash flow, to provide the resources for expansion, or to take on costly projects. New capital also becomes necessary when senior partners reach retirement age, if their departure from the firm requires a return of their capital.

Law firms have limitations in regard to supporting their financial needs. Because law firms in the United States are not allowed to have outside investors, those sources are limited to capital contributions of partners, loans from partners, loans from banks or from relatives, and loans in the form of leased equipment. Responsible financial management requires balancing all of those sources of money with capital contributions from existing and new partners as an important funding mechanism.

While there are a few large firms sufficiently successful to not require a capital contribution, most firms are set up to receive capital contributions from new partners. The amount of the capital contribution to be made by new partners should either be specified in the agreement or, better yet, based on a formula described in the agreement. Once a partner makes a capital contribution, that capital account is maintained, with periodic additions and subtractions until the partner's departure.

Many law firms are undercapitalized. Give consideration to your capital structure and consider retaining some earnings within the partnership to strengthen the firm's financial standing.

Voting

The partnership agreement should address several aspects of voting. For starters, the firm needs to decide whether to have per capita voting or weighted voting. Per capita means one vote per partner and is utilized by most partnerships. Weighted voting means that a partner's vote is weighted depending upon the partner's interest in the firm. For example, if the interest of partners A, B and C are 55 percent, 25 percent and 20 percent respectively, their votes would be weighted in those same proportions. In that simple example, partner A would control every majority vote based on a 55 percent interest in the firm. On the other hand, if an issue required a supermajority of two-thirds, partner A and one other partner could control the vote, but partners B and C could not control the vote, because their total interest in the firm is less than the two-thirds vote necessary.

This brings us to the consideration of majority votes and supermajority votes. A typical partnership agreement will set forth certain issues that will require more than a majority vote. The issues identified as requiring a supermajority vote of those deemed most significant and might include the admission of new partners, the purchase or sale of real estate, an offer of partnership, a merger, etc. Any issue not specified as requiring a supermajority vote would be decided based on a simple majority vote.

Management

Partnership agreements for relatively small firms will provide that the management of the firm is reserved to the partners to be delegated as they deem appropriate from time to time. Other partnership agreements may provide the basic provisions setting up a management committee structure or a managing partner structure. Regardless of the management approach adopted, care should be taken to make certain the partnership agreement remains free of unnecessary detail.

Profits

Profit distribution is a critical provision in a partnership agreement. While some firms describe in detail how profits will be allocated, it is a better course to create the structure in the partnership agreement and leave the detail to a vote of the partners. You don't want a partnership agreement that has to be amended every time there is a change in allocating the compensation.

The agreement may provide a broad general description of the allocation process; for example, the agreement may state that "the profits will be allocated based on a subjective system as determined by the partners from time to time." Or, the agreement may state that "the profits will be allocated based upon a formula as determined by the partners from time to time." The goal is for the partners to be able to amend the factors or adjust compensation, without requiring an amendment of the partnership agreement.

Retirement

Retirement can be voluntary or mandatory. Firms that have seen senior partners work into their 80s, with all the attendant risks, were the first to consider adopting mandatory retirement at a certain age. The mandatory retirement concept can be modified by a provision that allows for annual contracts after the retirement age, as determined by management on a case-by-case basis. In that circumstance, the partner who still brings great value to the firm can be retired from the partnership, under the mandatory retirement provision, and then enter into a one-year contract, subject to renewal, for a certain level of services on an annual basis. This is an excellent way to allow protection from the old partner who is both unproductive and a risk, while at the same time allowing the valuable lawyers to work beyond the mandatory retirement age at the firm's discretion.

Most firms have eliminated provisions for unfunded retirement benefits. The unfunded arrangements were simply agreements that the partnership would support retired partners from the earnings of the firm. Unfunded retirements were commonplace in the 1950s and 1960s but as firms grew, the challenges of producing adequate compensation for the working partners, as well as benefits for retired partners, made unfunded benefits unrealistic. In fact, some firms liquidated to get out from under oppressive retirement benefit commitments.

Currently, firms often limit the retiring partner to a return of capital and any benefits under a funded retirement plan. In the interest of fundamental fairness, transitions have been managed by allowing partners nearing retirement age to retire under the existing unfunded system, while putting in place funded retirement benefits for the younger partners.

Disability

One of the most difficult decisions unexpectedly forced on a partnership is how to handle compensation for the partner who becomes disabled. The partners' loyalties and instincts may be generous, but the financial strain on the partnership can be devastating. If the partnership agreement does not have a guiding provision, there will be intense pressure on the partners to continue paying the disabled partner irrespective of the firm's financial situation. Partners support each other and it may be perceived as unacceptable to cease compensation to a disabled partner.

The partnership agreement needs to specify the partnership's obligation to a disabled partner. There are a number of different approaches, some providing full compensation or partial compensation for a certain period of time. The important factor here is that all partners understand the rules going in. The firm may elect to provide disability insurance after a certain period, thereby limiting the firm's obligation. Other firms will leave it to the partners to select and pay for their own disability insurance, knowing that the commitment of the firm is limited.

The agreement should address temporary disability and permanent disability, with different provisions in terms of the compensation paid. In drafting the agreement, the partnership should also consider how disability determinations are going to be made. What if there is disagreement? How are disagreements resolved? It is safest to have a provision with a process for making these determinations, which frequently include acquiring a physician's opinion.

Death

If the partnership survives a partner's death, there needs to be a provision for paying the estate of the deceased partner its share of the value of the partnership. Does the estate of the deceased partner simply receive a return of capital invested or is the estate of the deceased partner entitled to receive its pro-rata share of the value of the partnership? If the plan is to employ the latter, then the question arises as to how the partnership is to be valued. Typical business appraisal methodology can be applied to a law partnership, but it may be better to provide a specific formula in the partnership agreement. The formula can address the specifics of a law business, such as how to treat work-in-process, receivables and contingency cases.

The final issue concerning a partner's death involves the right to continue using the deceased partner's name in the firm name. Assuming there are no local ethical rules to the contrary, most lawyers would prefer to continue the brand for marketing purposes rather than constantly changing the firm's name. A simple provision in the partnership agreement will give the remaining lawyers that choice.

Withdrawal

A partner's decision to withdraw from the firm raises similar questions concerning the value of the partnership interest. Some firms treat withdrawal the same as death or expulsion, while other firms create a disincentive by employing a different financial arrangement should a partner voluntarily withdraw. There is no requirement that a departing partner be treated the same, irrespective of the reason for the departure.

There are additional issues concerning the rights and duties of the partner to the firm after a decision has been made to depart. As long as the partner is a member of the firm, the partner owes the primary duty to the firm. It would be improper for the departing partner to give clients advance notice or lobby them to follow the departing partner to a new practice setting. The best way to manage a departure is to have the partners' rights and responsibilities clearly set forth in the partnership agreement to avoid uncertainty. Typical provisions include:

- The departing partner's duty to not to take any action that compromises the firm's interests.
- A requirement that the departing partners provide the other partners with a certain notice prior to any departure.
- The right of the remaining partners to accelerate the departure date should they deem it to be in the best interests of the firm.
- The specific requirement that a departing partner not notify any client of the intended departure prior to a joint letter signed by both the departing partner and a representative of the firm.
- The departing partner must provide the remaining partners with a sample letter to be provided to the clients of the departing partner outlining that the client has a choice of remaining with the firm or going with the departing partner.

Expulsion

A provision for expulsion of a partner is necessary to protect the partnership from a partner who is no longer willing or able to be a productive member of the group. For example, if a lawyer is disbarred and can no longer practice law, then that lawyer no longer qualifies to be a partner in a law partnership. The partnership agreement should provide that a disbarred lawyer is automatically expelled.

There may be other circumstances in which the partnership wants to clearly retain the discretionary right to expel a partner. To provide a basis for exercising that discretion, the partnership agreement should specify those circumstances that would give rise to possible expulsion. The circumstances could include bankruptcy, suspension from the practice of law, conviction of a crime, violation of the partnership agreement, or other actions that are harmful to the partnership. The expulsion of a partner is one of those issues that should be decided based on a supermajority vote and not a simple majority.

Under the circumstances, the partnership agreement needs to specify the nature of the notification to clients and the rights of the expelled partner to a return of capital and/or a payment for the expelled partner's interest in the firm.

Dissolution

The dissolution and liquidation of a law partnership needs to proceed in an orderly fashion to protect the rights of the firm's clients and the partners' interests. As might be expected, at a time of impending dissolution, the partners are often more focused on their individual career futures than in winding up the old partnership. To avoid a chaotic situation, the partnership agreement needs to specify the duties and responsibilities of each partner to the partnership in the dissolution process.

Step 2: Draft the Partnership Agreement

Take a look at the sample agreements in the Appendix which will include all of the critical provisions discussed. Except in larger firms, lawyers consider law firms to be partnerships in nature regardless of the entity structure. The substantive provisions will be essentially the same regardless of the entity structure. Appendix A is a Sample Long Form Partnership Agreement. Appendix B is a Sample Short Form Partnership Agreement. With regard to the professional association and the limited liability company, they are entities authorized by state law and care should be taken to make certain to fully comply with local law.[1]

---

[1]The Professional Association By-laws and the Limited Liability Company Operating Agreement will include the same operative provisions as set forth in the sample partnership agreements.

Streamlining Management

14

No law firm can afford to be poorly managed. Unlike the good ol' days when most lawyers survived pretty well, poorly managed firms now struggle until they ultimately implode or go out of business.

Step 1: Evaluate Current Management

Let's start by evaluating current management. To do that, ask the following questions:

- Does the firm have the appropriate management structure for current conditions?
- Do the people who manage the firm have the necessary skills and interest?
- Is the process efficient and effective, resulting in timely decisions?
- Do the firm leaders communicate effectively with the lawyers and staff?

Are the answers troublesome? If so, it may be that the firm's management structure is a relic of earlier times. It may be too cumbersome to be effective in current circumstances. The lawyers assigned to carry out the management functions may lack the necessary skills. Decisions may get bogged down in unruly and unnecessary processes. If the firm's management is below par, the firm is likely to be less profitable than better managed firms.

Step 2: Consider Changes to Firm Management

Changes to improve management will depend on where the firm is in its evolutionary process. For example, a first-generation firm with a founder who has been acting as managing partner since its inception faces very different issues than a firm that has already experienced changes in its management structure.

The First-Generation Law Firm

Discussion of a management transition in a first-generation law firm is often counter-intuitive and may appear to go against conventional wisdom. The cause of this non-traditional advice arises from the fact that most first-generation firms have had strong management from the firm's founder, which has resulted in a collection of lawyers who have been relieved of any management concern or responsibility. The partners have had a free ride and the firm may be made up of a full generation of partners without the necessary experience to take over the firm's management.

When the founder and managing partner announces a plan to retire, the first thought is who among the ranks is going to fill the founder's shoes and manage the firm going forward. There rarely is a candidate who has the talent, the demeanor, and the necessary respect of the other partners. The problem is compounded if the retiring founder has been an exceptional leader who has set the bar pretty high. No one should want to step into those shoes. Occasionally, there is one partner who wants the job, but the partner seeking it out usually is the wrong person for the leadership role.

Centralized management is desirable, except in this one situation. In a relatively small first-generation firm that has been run by a single individual, the other members of the firm lack an understanding of the business aspects of practicing law. There is a compelling need for a broader group participating in management, even if for only the educational experience.

Broader participation in management is achieved by shifting the management to an executive committee of three members with staggered terms. Each member of the executive committee can be assigned an area or primary responsibility (e.g., financial, human resources, building and equipment, etc.). The founder who wants to transition out of the managing partner role can be assigned the one-year slot on the committee and in that year act as Chair and help mentor the others in their new roles. The committee can start by meeting for an hour each week, with a formal agenda and a follow-up report circulated to all the partners. Once the committee gets up and running, a meeting every other week may be sufficient. See Appendix C for a job description for each of the management committee positions.

As the firm evolves, there will likely come a time when it transitions back to a managing partner structure. The committee will have served a valuable purpose in managing the firm through the critical transitions from the first generation to the second.

Centralized Management

Successful institutional firms have recognized the need to move to centralized management. In most circumstances, management by committees is outdated. The trend toward a managing partner is supported by the need to make decisions quickly in this fast-paced workplace, the need to develop management expertise, and the need to minimize the loss of billable time by focusing it on one lawyer. See Appendix D for a sample Managing Partner Job Description.

Increased Delegation

In addition to a more centralized management structure, it is important that the managing partner delegate as much work as reasonably possible to the firm's administrator and other staff.

Improved Communication

For the partners to accept a lesser role in management in favor of a more centralized approach, it is necessary to inspire the confidence of these partners. This requires effective communication so that the partners understand the issues, the decisions, and the plan going forward.

Conduct Fewer Meetings

Administrative meetings are a great robber of law firm profits. Not only do lawyers dislike administrative meetings, but they can be poorly run and ineffective in accomplishing results in an expeditious manner. Limit the number of meetings that partners must attend and make certain that the meetings that are held are effectively run and conclude in a timely manner.

Step 3: Address Problem Partners

Most firms have one or more problem partners who are either a drain on the firm's financial resources, a disruptive factor in the firm's operation, or a risk for committing malpractice. In some cases, these partners bring disrepute to the firm because of the public attention brought to their problem.

The Unproductive Partner

Managing partners and administrators admit, often discreetly, that an unproductive partner is the greatest financial drain on a law firm. Not only are unproductive partners a financial burden, but the failure to address the problem leads to a decline in partner morale, the morale of the firm at large, and undermines leadership credibility.

As firms struggle to adequately reward their top performers, increased focus has been directed at the unproductive partner. Cutting loose an unproductive partner was once thought to be a large-firm strategy. In today's world, no firm can afford to carry an unproductive partner; leadership must find a way to assist in making the partner productive or must be prepared to make the tough decision of encouraging a departure.

The Disruptive Partner

Many firms have lawyers who are difficult to get along with and make the workplace unbearable for others, if not the whole firm. Failure to take action against the disruptive partner results in penalizing people who get along with each other and work in a cooperative mode contributing to the firm's success. While the partner may make significant contributions to the firm's financial health, this is not a justifiable excuse for failing to take action and ignoring the fact that the disruptive partner is making the workplace insufferable for colleagues and staff.

Substance Abuse and Depression

Drug abuse, alcohol abuse, and depression present special problems in a law partnership. The tendency of law partners is to first be in denial and then later to tolerate the situation based on the partnership/marriage analogy, namely "for better or for worse."

The troubled partner will not be quick to admit to a problem and, in fact, may cover up the issue for as long as possible. Even when the problem is exposed, taking action is problematic for most partners, based on what may be inadequately defined partnership obligations. Most partners need to be reminded that their obligation to the firm's clients trumps any obligation to the troubled partner. Candid discussions are critical, as is quick intervention. Bar association intervention programs are but one of an increasing number of resources available to lawyers and law firms.

Step 4: Empower a Professional Administrator

The credentials of the law firm administrator will depend on the size of the firm. A small firm will have an administrator who handles limited matters under the close supervision of the managing partner or the executive committee. See Appendix E for a sample Small Firm Administrator's Job Description. A larger firm will have a professional administrator with different credentials and the ability to run the business side of the firm with limited supervision. See Appendix F for a sample Large Firm Administrator Job Description.

While it is important to expand the role and responsibility of the professional administrator, it is also necessary to know where to draw the line. Some firms have made the mistake of holding the administrator responsible for the partners' failings. For example, holding the administrator responsible for poor collections overlooks the lawyer's role of client intake, setting up the fee arrangement, and managing the client's expectation. At the end of the day, the administrator may have no control over the collection because of the arrangement with the client entered into by the lawyer. Lawyers should not delegate associate evaluations to the administrator. That is a lawyer job. The administrator should not have undue influence over the partner compensation process. The lawyers should control compensation with input from the administrator.

Developing Useful Management Reports

15

How useful is the financial information you and your partners review? Do you have the information you need? Do the partners understand the significance of the information they review? Is the information effective in helping manage the firm to greater success? For many firms, the answers to these questions reveal an inadequate reporting process.

The effectiveness of law firm financial software has more to do with how it is used, rather than what it is capable of doing. Too many bookkeepers in small firms use the financial software for the critical operative procedures, that is, managing payables, making payroll, and recording payments from clients. At year end, they produce a profit and loss (P&L) statement, a balance sheet, and 1099s, thinking their job is done. While these reports are essential and useful, they do not begin to provide the information needed to run a successful law firm.

The remarkable aspect of law firm financial software is the seemingly endless amount of information that can be analyzed, sorted, and displayed, if the bookkeeper knows what information is desired and what needs to be done to get it from the program. Unfortunately, unless your bookkeeper is well experienced in the financial aspects of running a law firm, he or she will not know enough to take the initiative and produce the reports you need. The solution is twofold: first, let your bookkeeper know the type of information you require and, second, authorize outside help, if necessary, from professionals who have a complete understanding of the software. All but the most computer-savvy individuals need help configuring the software to maximize the information available.

Step 1: Determine What Data You Want to Know

You will want to consider the need for financial data, whether it is to have a firm focus, as well as similar data sorted by practice group, individual partner (or responsible lawyer),[1] and some reports by associate and paralegal. Consider the following:

For the Firm

- *Balance sheet.* The balance sheet will provide the firm's financial health and disclose assets and liabilities, including any short- or long-term debt. The balance sheet will alert the partners to any decline in the firm's value. It is normally checked at year end, but can be evaluated at any time during the year.
- *P&L statement.* The firm should have an annual budget against which the P&L statement can be compared. The P&L statement should be reviewed monthly to get an early warning if there is a shortfall of revenue developing, or if there are excessive expenses that are not reflected in the budget.
- *Billable hours report.* Each timekeeper's billable hours should be checked at the end of each month. The hours report is the earliest warning of a potential revenue problem that will surface a couple months later. If the shortfall is because of lack of work, the practice group's leader may be able to shift work to make everyone productive. If the shortfall is due to insufficient support, corrective action can be taken. Address hour shortfall immediately to limit the impact later on.
- *Billing report.* Watch the monthly billings report. A lower than expected number for any partner signals either lack of work or a delay in billings. Get on the issue quickly and provide the support necessary to get the bills out without delay.
- *Aged work-in-process.* If you see an individual's work in process building for no legitimate reason, it signals poor billing habits. Make sure the partner is reminded of the need to bill regularly and in a timely manner.
- *Billing realization.* Track the amount of time that is being written off and, if at an unacceptable level, examine the reasons and take corrective action.

---

[1] It is critical to good financial management and to creating proper incentives, to measure results by responsible lawyer, which means the lawyer (usually a partner) who has responsibility for managing a file gets credit for the hours and the amounts billed and paid on the file by other partners, associates and paralegals. Giving credit for successful delegation and management is important, as is making the responsible lawyer accountable for write-downs, write-offs and collection problems.

■ *Cash receipts.* Cash receipts are what counts. You can't pay the rent with hours or billings. Make sure your receipts track the previous month's billings. If there is an unexplained drop off, get on it quickly.

■ *Aged receivables.* Your receivables should be sorted by age. Make your focus the sixty-day column and take action while the receivables are relatively fresh. For management purposes, establish and age (perhaps twelve months) and automatically remove receivables from the list and place them in the doubtful accounts category.

■ *Doubtful accounts.* Doubtful accounts are those receivables that are no longer counted on for revenue projections and have been moved to a separate category for collection efforts.

■ *Collection realization.* Track the average percent of billings that are collected and if the collection realization is unacceptable, initiate more aggressive collection efforts.

■ *Disbursements.* Management should track carefully client disbursements from month to month and make certain that they are billed and recovered at the earliest possible time.

For Responsible Lawyers

■ *Billing report.* The firm should track the total billings of each partner, which will reflect the dollars charged by the associates and paralegals working on the partner's files. The total amount of work managed by each partner is a relevant number to track.

■ *Billing realization.* Partners need to be held accountable for any write-offs of associate and paralegal time.

■ *Aged work-in-process.* This report will monitor how well the partners are billing out their own hours and the hours of associates and paralegals working on their files.

■ *Cash receipts.* The cash receipts report will track the revenue production of each partner for the matters they are managing.

■ *Collection realization.* Partners need to be held accountable for the failure to collect billed associate and paralegal time.

■ *Utilization report.* A utilization report is a grid showing how many hours each associate and paralegal invests on the files of each partner. It is useful in evaluating and managing associate and paralegal support.

■ *Disbursements.* Disbursements should be sorted by responsible partner to facilitate billing and collection efforts.

For Associates and Paralegals

■ *Billable hours report.* Associates and paralegals should be evaluated based on the number of billable hours and the quality of their work. They should not be evaluated on dollars billed, as they have no control over client in-take or write-offs.

For Practice Groups

The management of a practice group involves the review of the following reports sorted by individual practice groups.

- **Billing report.** Track practice group billing. A positive trend may signal a growing practice area with a need for additional resources. A decline may show the opposite, a reduction in work available, and a possible need for downsizing the group.
- **Aged work-in-process.** Make sure the lawyers are billing out their time on a regular basis. Delays in billing result in poor collections.
- **Billing realization.** Billing realization will reflect the adequacy of the intake policies, the effectiveness of delegation, and the quality of associate and paralegal work.
- **Cash receipts.** Cash receipts should be measured against the practice group's revenue budget. Tracking receipts on a monthly basis gives the practice group an opportunity to make changes and improve results.
- **Aged receivables.** Watching aged receivables can signal changes in the quality of the practice group's clients and the attention of its lawyers to collection efforts.
- **Collection realization.** Tracking write-offs provides the firm with information necessary to evaluate whether to continue working in the practice area or reduce the volume and retain only the better cases.
- **Utilization report.** The utilization report allows management to track which associates and paralegals work for which partners. It provides useful information when considering the hiring or firing of associates or paralegals.

Step 2: Evaluate the Purpose of the Reports

How will the reports be used? Well, for starters, you want to be able to manage the firm, make projections, and have early warning of any threats to the firm's financial health. You also want all partners to understand and appreciate the significance of their actions, and you want to incentivize desirable behaviors. Lawyers want to look good on the financial reports, so the strategic decision on what to circulate can be an effective management tool.

Step 3: Create Meaningful Summaries

Partners in law firms, large and small, get a set of financial reports at the end of every month. In larger firms, the reports are a stack of documents, sometimes over an inch thick. These distributions satisfy the need to openly share information with all partners; however, in many situations, the reports have little significance to the lawyers. The partners either have a limited ability to interpret the significance of the numbers, or they get in the habit of only looking at the portion of the numbers that they think make them look good.

Management should prepare a one-page summary of the critical financial indicators that are tracked each month. See Appendix G. In addition, the managing partner should prepare a one-page cover sheet with a one-paragraph summary of the significance of the reported data. See Appendix H. Attach the one-page summary and the cover sheet to the stack of data, thereby giving the partners the option of only reading and absorbing the summary or looking at all the detailed reports.

Reviewing the Partner Compensation System | **16**

Compensation is always a touchy subject, but healthy firms are not afraid to discuss it in partner meetings or retreat sessions. During the formation of a partnership, the soon-to-be partners must determine a method for sharing profits. The agreement may operate successfully for years, perhaps decades, but as the firm grows, that start-up method of dividing profits may no longer serve the firm or its lawyers well. Yet, partners may struggle along with increased levels of discontent and a reluctance to take the risk of disruption by attempting to change a core concept central to the partner relationship.

Keeping the firm stable and the partners from looking for other opportunities requires constant attention to the partner compensation process. As a result, firm leaders need to be sensitive to any underlying dissatisfaction with the system or the process.

For purposes of this discussion, the steps listed below will guide firms that need to re-evaluate and/or make changes to their partner compensation system.

Step 1: Understand the Core Principles

Keep in mind the five core principles of a healthy partner compensation system:

- The system needs to reflect the values and the goals of the partners.

- The manner of setting compensation must be perceived as fair and resulting in a reasonable division of profits.
- The system should reward desired behaviors and not reward unwanted behaviors.
- The partners need to have a process available that encourages candid and open discussion about compensation.
- The compensation system should be reviewed and re-evaluated by the partners in a retreat setting at least every five years.

Step 2: Evaluate the Present Compensation System

The managing partner needs to assess the nature of issues relating to the partner compensation system before deciding how to proceed. The possibilities include:

- The compensation system appears to be working well, but a review of the system is necessary to remind longstanding partners of how it works and to ensure that the most recently admitted partners have a full understanding of how the system works.
- There may be some question as to the fairness or appropriateness of the operation of the compensation system and the firm needs to provide partners with a forum for a candid discussion.
- The compensation system has served the firm well, but there may be emerging issues which suggest that some modification may be in the firm's best interest.
- There are increased tensions among partners that demonstrate the compensation system needs to be re-evaluated and possibly changed.
- The present compensation system creates the wrong incentives and is no longer serving in the firm's best interest.

The approach for tweaking a system that is periodically reviewed and has worked well will be different from the approach necessary if the compensation system is deemed to require a major review and overhaul.

Step 3: Consider a Partner Compensation System Study Committee

Some firms establish a special committee to conduct a comprehensive study of the firm's compensation and prepare a written report making recommendations for change after conducting research, inclusive of interviewing all of the partners. The study and the committee's recommendations would then be delivered to the partners and discussed at a retreat, normally requiring at least a half-day at an off site location.

There are differing approaches to such a review, and the amount of preparation preceding the retreat may vary, depending on the circumstances. Nevertheless, the standard process would include:

- At least four months before the retreat date, announce to the partners by memo that the firm's annual retreat will involve a review and evaluation of the firm's partner compensation system. Attach to the memo the written description of the current system and any articles or other information you want your partners to review and consider. See Appendix I for a Sample Memo.

- The next step is for one or two committee members to conduct interviews with each partner to appreciate their respective views of the issues at hand. The suggestions and opinions expressed in the interviews will be synthesized and presented as part of a report to the partners, with the individual views of each partner remaining anonymous. See Appendix J for a Sample Outline of Questions.

- The written report should include a brief discussion of the operation of the existing system, a summary of the differing views of the partners, the conclusions of the committee, and the recommendations. See Appendix K for a Sample Report Table of Contents.

- The written report should be circulated in advance of the retreat and firm leadership should plan to present and discuss the report and its conclusions at the retreat. See Appendix L for a Sample Retreat Agenda.

Step 4: Hold a Retreat on Partner Compensation

After the committee has studied the matter, polled individuals, and made recommendations, the retreat is a vehicle for discussing and adopting recommendations. If the firm is proceeding without the advance work of a committee, however, firm leadership will need to guide the partners through an evaluation of the existing compensation system and build a consensus for change.

- This approach achieves the best results when the discussion leader starts by getting agreement on the firm's values and its objectives. It is always easier to build from the bottom (core values) up, rather than jumping right into the specifics during which the partners will more easily see the ramifications to their own individual situations.

- Once the core values and objectives are determined, the next discussion point is finding the kind of compensation system that best reflects the core values and best promotes the objectives.
- With a decision made about the system, the next issue is to determine what factors will be considered (whether a formula or subjective)
- What will the process be? Who will do what?

With this approach, it is critical that the retreat facilitator be neutral on the issues with no personal agenda. While a firm leader might serve as the facilitator, an outside consultant may better preserve the need for neutrality in most situations.

Step 5: Making Compensation Systems Work

Selecting a workable partner compensation system is an important step, but equally important is defining the process and then making sure it is understood by all partners and considered fair. Each system is vulnerable to failure in application, so constant vigilance is necessary.

Equality Compensation System

- *Be sensitive to any perceived unfairness.* The firm's leaders and managers need to be attentive to any concern that the system is already unfair or may be heading in that direction. It may be important to have a culture that allows for open and candid discussions of the issue. In fact, a discussion at an annual retreat would provide an ideal forum.
- *Maintain good financial records.* The partners need to have continued confidence that sharing profits equally is fair. To make that judgment, be sure to have a good set of monthly financial reports that reflect each aspect of financial performance.
- *Share firm management burdens.* Provide for each partner to participate in some aspect of non-billable functions so that there will be a fair division of those responsibilities.

Lock-Step Compensation System

- *Be sensitive to any perceived unfairness.* The firm's leaders and managers need to be attentive to any concern that the system is already unfair or may be heading in that direction. It may be important to have a culture that allows for open and candid discussions of the issue. In fact, a discussion at an annual retreat would provide an ideal forum.

- ***Maintain good financial records.*** The partners need to have continued confidence that sharing profits equally is fair. To make that judgment, be sure to have a good set of monthly financial reports that reflect each aspect of financial performance.
- ***Share firm management burdens.*** Provide for each partner to participate in some aspect of non-billable functions so that there will be a fair division of those responsibilities.

Formula Compensation System

- ***Make sure every partner understands the system.*** While this advice seems obvious, there are reported instances where the formula was so complicated that some partners did not understand how compensation was calculated and were afraid to ask.

Find a way to compensate for management activities and other needed contributions to the firm that cannot be measured by revenue produced. See Appendix M for Sample Formula System.

Subjective Compensation System

- ***Have accurate data.*** A subjective system involves the general consideration of the financial performance of each partner. To make those subjective judgments, it is necessary to have complete and accurate information. Trouble abounds if there is a sense that the data circulated in unreliable.
- ***Make sure the factors to be considered are understood.*** Don't let the process be a mystery because one of more of the partners may not know what factors the committee is considering. The process needs to be completely transparent.
- ***Follow an agreed to and published process.*** Subjective systems work best when there is a high level of trust among the partners. The partners need to know who decides on compensation and the exact process involved to reach the result. See Appendix N for Sample Subjective System.

Step 6: Consider a Partner Evaluation Process

Some firms have been slow to develop a partner evaluation process. The idea seems contrary to the autonomy that most lawyers desire and cling to at all costs. As a result, it needs to be broached carefully. In some firms, the process is centered on the development of individual lawyer practice plans.

The evaluation process has at least two goals. First of all, it provides a mechanism for the compensation committee to provide constructive criticism to help each lawyer improve his or her level of contribution to the firm's success. In addition, the practice plans provide a standard by which the compensation committee can determine each partner's relative worth to the firm.

The evaluation process would start near the end of a calendar year and would go something like this:

Partner Profile

Each partner would fill out a partner profile form which would seek information about the individual's personal productivity and contributions to the firm during the current year. It presents an opportunity for each partner to point to contributions that may not be well recognized or noticed.

The partner profile form would also ask what additional contributions the partner can make in the coming year. One member of the management committee (or compensation committee) meets with each partner to review and discuss the information on the partner profile forms. See Sample Partner Profile at Appendix O.

Committee Review

The committee responsible for the evaluation process meets to review the partner profile forms and discuss any other matters learned as a result of the individual meetings with partners.

The Evaluation

The committee will next evaluate each partner and craft an evaluation message which will take the form of a narrative description of the partner's strengths and areas for improvement. See Sample Evaluation Form at Appendix P.

Annual Plan

The committee member will then meet with each partner to deliver the evaluation and work with the partner to develop an annual plan for the partner. The annual plan should address changes in practice areas, plans to expand their practice or improve their skills, efforts to train and mentor others, assumption of responsibilities within the firm, any civic or professional participation, and other ways of contributing to the advancement of the firm's goals. Finally, the plan should include expectations with regard to billable hours, fees billed, and realization achieved. The agreed to plan should be in writing and should be signed by both the partner and the committee member. The annual plan will play a prominent role in the following year's evaluation, as the partner will be reviewed on the basis of whether the commitments in the plan are met. See Sample Partner

Annual Plan Worksheet at Appendix Q and Sample Partner Annual Plan at Appendix R.

This annual planning process focuses each lawyer on an individual plan that has been jointly developed by the lawyer in discussion with firm leadership. To the extent the lawyers can accomplish the plans set out for them, the firm benefits from the coordinated approach designed to achieve firm goals. At the same time, the partner compensation committee can look at how each lawyer has worked towards the agreed-to plan, in evaluating their contribution to the firm's success.

Developing a More Productive Professional Staff **17**

The hallmark of a successfully functioning firm is a capable and well-integrated professional staff composed of the proper mix of associates and paralegals who work well together in effectively advancing the clients' objectives. A productive professional staff is the result of good training and mentoring in the context of an effective working model.

The recruiting and hiring of associates and paralegals is an important step towards achieving the goal, but only a first step. Without a carefully constructed plan, most new associates and paralegals will eventually be a disappointment to the partnership. Only about 10 percent of new lawyers have the internal wherewithal to achieve success without good training and mentoring. The vast majority of new associates and paralegals require focused attention to achieve their potential within the firm.

In addition to more stable support and client service, associate and paralegal retention is a critical component of a financially healthy firm. The generally accepted rule of thumb is that turnover costs the firm between two and three times the individual's salary. A managing partner of a fifty-lawyer firm in New Jersey conducted a study that concluded that the turnover cost of an associate in his firm was approximately $300,000. That number was reached by adding up the cost of recruiting, training, and lost billings from duplication of work in transitioning associates on client files. Many firms have unknowingly suffered serious financial difficulty caused by associate turnover.

Step 1: Make Good Hiring Decisions

Start by thinking broadly about the choices. Does the firm need to hire a lawyer, or could the work be performed by a paralegals working under the supervision of a lawyer? Given a choice, most firms would opt for an experienced paralegal. But the analysis does not end there. Give thought to whether the addition will be permanent or temporary. If you are hiring only to service the needs of one client with a big case, give consideration to hiring a contract lawyer or a freelance paralegal. The advantage would be that temporary employment can be terminated when the matter concludes. Avoid adding to permanent payroll if the need may be temporary.

In considering whether to hire an associate or a paralegal, look at each professional's respective skills and talents.

An associate:

- Knows the law or how to find it
- Desires to learn from the partner
- May lack experience
- Wants to be a valuable associate
- Wants to be considered for partnership

A paralegal:

- Has practical skills
- Knows office procedures
- Knows legal procedures
- Has case management skills
- Provides good client service
- Understands partner expectations

Most associates are in training to become partners. They will serve in a support role for a limited period of time. A paralegal will never be a partner and career paralegals will provide long-term support.

There are other key differences. The associate will be able to cover a court hearing or conduct complex legal research. If those services are needed, an associate should be hired. If the support role does not involve court hearings and complex research, however, consider hiring a paralegal. Paralegals tend to be more thorough and detail oriented, which means they excel at case management and client relations.

Before hiring an associate, prepare a summary of what qualities the firm needs. As part of that exercise, think about the firm's successful associates and identify the characteristics that make an associate successful. Select a person with similar characteristics. Think about the firm's culture. Is it hard driving or laid back? Some diversity of work ethic is acceptable, but a seriously fractured culture is always problematic. Be attentive to the firm's values. If hard work and long hours are standard, avoid hiring associates with a professed lifestyle focus. If originating new clients is important to your firm, look for individuals with an entrepreneurial spirit. Take the time to make the right selection.

If the decision is to hire one or more paralegals, start with an understanding of the role and the talents and skills necessary to perform the needed services. Make sure the candidate is one who can work with the lawyer and, most important, engender the lawyer's confidence. Take a hard look at whether to hire an entry-level paralegal or an experienced paralegal. Unless the work to be performed is basic or the lawyer for whom the paralegal will work is good at mentoring, it may be a mistake to hire an inexperienced paralegal. Avoid individuals whose commitment to the paralegal profession seems limited. Many individuals pass though the paralegal profession as a resting place until they figure out what they really want to do later on. Look for career paralegals. As discussed in Chapter 9, greater profits can often be achieved from the work of an experienced paralegal.

Step 2: Improve Associate Training

A well-designed and properly implemented associate training program will pay huge dividends. There are two sides to the issue. First, develop a training plan that will assure that associates get up to speed quickly and are able to bring value to their client service effort. In this market, sophisticated clients are skeptical about paying high associate rates when associates are learning their way through a case at the client's expense. Equally important is the goal of making associates feel as if the firm is committed to helping them develop as effective lawyers with a career plan. Associate turnover is expensive, but even worse is the fact that the associates with the best potential will be the first to go. If you don't have an associate training program, develop one.

The associate training program should be managed by a lawyer assigned to that role or consider appointing a committee, if the firm has more than ten associates. The lawyer or committee in charge of the program should be supported by the firm's administrator, who can take on many of the duties. Some firms look to one or more experienced paralegals to have a role in the program.

Orientation

Law schools do not prepare their graduates for the complexities of the workplace or working in an office setting. To ensure an associate gets off to a successful start, the law firm needs a thoughtful, organized, and phased approach to orientation.

The orientation should include

- Office tour
- Salary and benefit information
- Associate evaluations, salary reviews, and partnership criteria
- Associate training and CLE policy
- Rules of professional responsibility and trust accounting
- Secretarial and administrative support
- Policies and procedures
- Practice management
- Timekeeping, calendaring, and docket control
- Filing systems
- Billing procedures
- Financial aspects of a law firm
- Firm management

The session leaders may change, depending on the subject matter, and the information is best presented in two-hour sessions over a period of a couple of weeks. The information is best absorbed if it is spread out in digestible chunks. See Appendix S for a Sample Orientation Program.

Mentoring

Mentoring is a critical component of developing successful lawyers. Unfortunately, most firms have difficulty getting their partners to take the time to effectively mentor the firm's associates. The best mentoring success stories involve matches of partners and associates that develop naturally, rather than in response to a compulsory mentoring program.

The mentor's role is often described as someone that:

- Helps the associate understand the workings of the firm
- Can be a confidante and good listener
- Guides the associate with personal or office related problems
- Is willing to be an advocate for the associate or provide balance to any discussion

- Assists the associate with career plans
- Joins the associate at bar association and community events
- Socializes and becomes a friend

A fundamental question is whether the mentor should be a lawyer with whom the associate works regularly. Some would advocate that the close working relationship makes for an ideal mentor–mentee relationship. The better view is to have a more neutral and objective mentor, someone who is removed from day-to-day work. The mentor is then in a position to assist, should the difficult issue involve the supervising partner, which often can be the case.

Unfortunately, the increased cost of providing legal services to clients has affected many firms' commitment to time-consuming mentoring programs. Firms committed to making a mentoring program work will include mentoring as one of the factors considered in setting partner compensation. Compensation is always the ultimate management tool. See Appendix T for a Sample Mentoring Program.

Training

Gone are the days of rotating new associates through several departments in six-month intervals to expose them to each area of the law. Regardless of their eventual practice specialty, the rotation made associates better lawyers because it gave them a broad understanding of several areas of the law. Unfortunately, the high associate salaries have made it impossible for most firms to give their associates a two-year training rotation before having them select the practice area they decide to pursue.

Opportunities for learning by doing or watching others have diminished as clients are insisting on clear value for the hours they pay for. At the same time, high associate salaries put pressure on law firms to bill out every associate hour they can find. These competing dilemmas have resulted in most firms hiring new associates for specific practice areas and getting them billing as many hours as possible. Old timers will say the new associates will never be as good because of their limited training and narrow focus.

There is another aspect to this issue. As associates get thrown into narrow practice areas, they will not be capable of picking up work in other areas, should the need arise to assist lawyers in other practice areas who may become overloaded. From a financial vantage point, having lawyers who are versatile will allow the shifting of work from time to time, which will result in better profits. While rotation of practice areas may be out of the question, give consideration to making it possible for each associate to develop some ability to work in a second practice area.

An associate training program should include:

- Monitoring a task performance list for associates in the practice area
- Developing a secondary task performance list for other associates to learn the basics in each practice area
- Provide in-house CLEs
- Allow attendance at CLEs by outside providers
- Adopt an associate training hours policy

Making sure all associates in the practice area can learn by performing all of the tasks set out on a list is a good way to ensure each associate in the practice area attains a certain level of experience in learning by doing. Some firms develop a shorter list for each practice area to guide them in some level of cross training. See Appendix U for a Sample Associate Performance List.

In addition to on the job experience, CLEs are critical. In-house CLEs and outside CLEs provide different types of information and each has their place in a well-designed associate training program.

Many firms have developed an associate training hours' policy, which is designed to give all associates some opportunity to learn by watching partners practice law. For example, such a policy might be that associates in their first two years of practice have annual billable hour commitments of eighteen hundred hours, but three hundred of those hours can be training hours, which do not need to be billed to the client. To operate under such a policy, firm management must be prepared to see only fifteen hundred billable hours from each associate in his or her first two years. This can be an effective way to provide necessary experience to your associates, without requiring your clients to pay for the time and without the risk of ramifications therefrom. See Appendix V for a Sample Associate Training Policy.

Step 3: Conduct Associate and Paralegal Evaluations

Partners need to understand that timely feedback on each assignment is the best way to help associates and paralegals improve their work. At the same time, partners have a reluctance to provide individual feedback, particularly if it is negative. Too many partners internalize their disappointment and never choose to work with the associate or paralegal again. Those same partners know that is not the most productive approach but given the disappointment, busy schedules, and the discomfort in facing the need to criticize an associate, they simply ignore the issue and move on to the next client problem.

Every firm needs a formal associate and paralegal evaluation process. Evaluation forms should be completed by all partners who have worked with the individual associate or paralegal. The form should highlight the level of work performed by the individual for the partner, keeping in mind more weight should be given to the evaluation results of those partners who work the most with the person being evaluated. In many respects, the areas of inquiry for associates will be similar to the areas of inquiry for paralegals. The following subjects should be covered:

Associates	**Paralegals**
■ Competence	■ Competence
■ Communication skills	■ Communication skills
■ Writing ability	■ Writing ability
■ Problem-solving ability	■ Problem-solving ability
■ Professionalism	■ Reliability
■ Reliability	■ Client relations
■ Client relations	■ Loyalty and dedication
■ Loyalty and dedication	
■ Community activities	
■ Marketing potential	
■ Partnership potential (by third year)	

The individual partner or the committee responsible for the associate evaluations should synthesize the information obtained in the process and craft a message to the associate which describes the results of the evaluation. The message should be delivered in a discussion format, but a written copy of the message should be delivered to the associate, with a copy filed in the associate's personnel file. A copy of the message will be useful a year later when evaluating whether the associate has made improvements in the areas designated. See Appendix W for a Sample Associate Evaluation Form.

Step 4: Focus on Career Planning for Associates

If your goal is associate retention, there is no issue more important to associates than providing an understanding of the firm's long-term opportunities. Most associates do not have the insight or the tools necessary to put a career plan in place. As a result, associates may resign from firms for the wrong reasons and with limited information. As partners in the firm, you should control which associates stay and which ones go. For too many firms, the decision making is reversed.

Step 5: Adopt Partnership Criteria

Effective associate programs include a clear message about what it takes to become a partner in the firm. Serious career-oriented candidates for the position of associate will ask the question. An unclear response or a blank look will tell the candidate more than you will want them to know about the firm. In particular, the partners in small to mid-sized firms often have not articulated the partnership criteria. By not having an answer to the question, you will eliminate the best candidates. See Appendix X for Sample Partnership Criteria.

Developing the Practice Groups 18

Effective practice management has become a critical component to the financial success of law firms, resulting in the increased importance of effective and well-run practice groups. These groups are segments of the lawyers, paralegals, and staff grouped together for the primary purpose of facilitating optimal client service in a given practice area. They can be large or small, and their specific focus will vary depending on the needs of the law firm and their clients. The groups can be organized according to areas of the law, a specific industry or client, or a type of service.

A small to mid-sized firm will have practice groups that cover the basic areas of the law in which they provide service: Real Estate Practice Group, Estate Planning and Probate Practice Group; Business Law Practice Group; and Litigation Practice Group. Larger firms may develop a department structure covering the basic areas, with several more narrowly defined practice groups within each department.

Depending on the firm's client mix, it may make sense to have practice groups focused on a specific industry or client. For example, a firm with a significant component of utility work might have a Water Company Practice Group. Instead of limiting the groups to an area of the practice, it would incorporate all legal areas typically handled for water companies, including corporate counseling, employment advice, real estate transactions, environmental issues, public utilities proceedings, and litigation. Similarly, if the firm has a major client that requires the integration of a number of practice areas, the firm might have a practice group dedicated to one client.

For smaller firms with no formal practice groups, considering this structure can take place at any time. The initial goals for taking that step will be to encourage a higher degree of specialization, allow a forum for sharing information, provide more coordinated services, improve the quality of the work, and track the practice area's profits to the firm. For those firms with some type of practice group structure, it is necessary to re-evaluate its operation and make needed improvements over time. And finally, as practice groups evolve, the practice group leaders should provide support to firm management by taking a role in monitoring and managing the revenue goals of the practice group.

Step 1: Decide What Groups Make Sense

The development of practice groups is an evolutionary process. If the firm has never operated with practice groups, select groups based on basic practice areas and begin to develop a coordinated approach to the delivery of legal services in those practice areas. The checklists in the appendices will provide a starting point for selecting initial goals for these start-up groups.

Start by determining the firm's strengths based on the resources in place, and compare the result to the needs of the marketplace the firm serves. Take a look at the profitability of each type of work performed by the firm and then assimilate the information to develop a strategic plan. The make-up of the practice groups should be designed to support the firm's future direction.

If your firm already has some type of practice groups, don't make the mistake of thinking there is no work to be done. Reflect on the goal's vision and goals. Have your lawyers come together, perhaps in a retreat session, and create a vision or a common direction for the firm going forward. It may be that the firm's practice group structure has reflected the firm's historical path. The goal as you look forward, however, is to reconsider and utilize the practice groups as a management tool to lead the firm into the future. Address these questions: Are the groups effective? Do the practice group leaders run meetings that are considered valuable by its members and firm management? Should there be a change in leadership or in the role of the practice group within the firm's management structure?

Step 2: Select the Leader

First and foremost, the chair of the practice group has to be chosen carefully, so that the group has the best opportunity to be useful to the firm. It has to be someone with leadership qualities who is organized, profitable, has the time and interest to perform the job, and succeeds at achieving the firm's hourly or revenue goals. Usually, the best candidate is a mid-level partner, not the most senior partner, and not the most successful partner, nor the firm's best rainmaker. Commonly, a less experienced partner is named secretary to the practice group and in that role provides support, while being mentored for a future leadership role. Finally, the practice group leader needs to be someone who has the skill to run a good meeting with an open discussion of the issues, but also knows how to control an agenda and the clock. Failure on this last point can be most painful.

Step 3: Determine the Purpose of Practice Groups

The primary goal of practice groups is to position the firm to provide better service to its clients. Once that goal is achieved, practice group leaders may become involved in managing workloads and then ultimately provide assistance to firm management in taking responsibility for achieving the group's revenue goal. The responsibilities grow with the size of the firm. The list of typical activities can be long.

Coordinating for Improved Delivery of Client Services

Practice group meetings are usually held monthly and attended by lawyers, paralegals, and sometimes support staff. The activities intended to improve the delivery of legal service include:

- *Review of new files.* Reviewing new files provides an expanded conflict's check to be sure there aren't policy type conflicts or issues not exposed by a technical computer conflict check. Further, lawyers and paralegals become aware of files involving similar issues which can result in sharing information and resources. And, if there are difficult issues presented, the responsible lawyer may benefit from a group discussion of the problem.
- *Practice group projects.* Creating forms, checklists, project plans, tickler systems, docket control, etc., are an important part of a practice group's effort to make the delivery of services more efficient and effective. Standardization of forms and procedure manuals can greatly improve the efficiency and the productivity of the lawyers and paralegals in a practice group setting. The group's meetings provide the forum to discuss needed projects, assign responsibilities, and monitor progress.
- *Current issues and problems.* The practice group meeting is a proper forum for any lawyer or paralegal to raise an issue and seek the input or advice of others. The issue raised could involve a ques-

tion of client management, a difficult issue of substantive law, a question of trial strategy, an attitude of a particular judge, or inquiry into the reliability of an opposing counsel. Problems can be solved, while at the same time educating and broadening the awareness of the less experienced lawyers.

■ *Training and development.* Experienced practice group members can make educational presentations designed to train and educate less experienced members. A series of short presentations on limited issues can be an effective associate development tool.

■ *Paralegal programs.* Paralegals are used differently, depending on the practice area. As a result, each practice group should be responsible for creating its own paralegal program, to include hiring criteria, job descriptions, guidelines for appropriate use, and an evaluation process. One lawyer within the practice group should have responsibility for the program.

■ *CLE reports.* Practice group meetings provide an opportunity for lawyers and paralegals who have attended outside CLE programs to share what they have learned with other members of the firm. In some situations, approval of a CLE request is conditioned on the individual sharing the high points of what was learned with others in the firm.

■ *Other informational matters.* The list of possibilities seems endless. Other informational matters can be discussed, including pending legislation, recent appellate decisions, new library acquisitions, relevant bar association activities, other community events, etc.

Marketing and Client In-take

The next phase in the development of a practice group is to get involved in the marketing of its services. As firms grow and develop diverse practices, the best marketing plans are those tailored to and focused on specific areas of the law. While there needs to be an overall firm vision, the specific marketing activities are different from one practice area to another. The practice groups should consider:

■ *Practice group marketing plans.* Under the direction of the managing partner, and within the prescribed budgetary limitations, the practice groups should develop and recommend a marketing plan which involves both attention to existing clients and the targeting of potential clients. This is based on the assumption that the lawyers practicing in the area are best able to determine how to spend their approved marketing budget.

■ *Individual marketing plans.* Each individual should develop a marketing plan which is consistent with and a component of the practice group's broader plan. The practice group leaders, or a marketing person, should have responsibility to assist the individual lawyers in creating and carrying out their plans.

Assisting Management on Financial Goals

As firms grow, practice groups mature and take on revenue responsibilities to assist firm management in monitoring the profitability aspects of the group and its members.

How involved the practice group leaders become in the financial aspects depends on the size of the firm and the approach to the issue taken by firm management. However, as firms grow, they reach a stage where practice groups need to take on responsibility for their own profitability. Here are some of the aspects undertaken:

- **Client in-take.** Client in-take is at the very heart of profitability. Most profitability issues can be traced back to clients that should not have been accepted, the remedy for which is better client in-take standards. Setting forth the guidelines and procedures for client in-take is practice group focused. Each practice group should have its own set of standards and procedures to ensure a more profitable practice.

- **Resources and support.** Practice group leaders are often given responsibility for managing the resources in their group and the staff support required by their lawyers and paralegals. This role starts with the leader having the goal of spreading out the workload within the practice groups to be sure maximum productivity is received from each member. The practice group leader would also be the individual assigned the task of evaluating support for the lawyers and paralegals and recommending changes.

- **Revenue budget.** When management works on its revenue budget, it will often consult with practice group chairs to either learn what revenue might be anticipated from the group, or, in the alternative, to discuss the group's potential and then come to some negotiated agreement as to the practice group's revenue goal for the year. Once set, the practice group leader has responsibility for monitoring and managing the group's resources to achieve the revenue anticipated.

- **Lawyer and paralegal evaluations.** The practice group leader should have a significant role in the evaluation process of partners, associates and paralegals, and have significant input into the salaries set for associates and paralegals. There should be a process for developing annual practice plans, under the guidance of the practice group leader, and a periodic review of the annual plans in connection with the firm's lawyer evaluation process. Depending upon the partner compensation system, the practice group leader may have input in to the allocation process.

■ ***Billing methods.*** Hourly billing is often not fair to clients or their lawyers. There is no predictability to hourly legal fees and the unexpected bills frequently damage the lawyer—client relationship. More and more, lawyers are being asked by their clients to quote flat fees or some alternative method. To accommodate these needs, lawyers need to learn how to price services in innovative ways. These efforts usually take place in pilot programs within the practice groups. (For more information on alternative billing methods, see *Winning Alternatives to the Billable Hour: Strategies that Work*, Third Edition by Mark A. Robertson and James A. Calloway (ABA, 2008).)

Step 4: Establish the Process

The next step is to decide the group's make-up and how it will function. In some firms, lawyers, paralegals, and all support members attend monthly meetings. In other firms, the meetings involve only lawyers and paralegals. Keep in mind that special guests, such as experts on relevant subjects, as well as in-house guests, should be considered. The meetings should be kept informative and progressive and attendees should look forward to the meetings as an opportunity to learn from one another on topics that the group has in common.

The meeting agenda is normally prepared by the secretary, with the assistance of the group's chair. The topics on the agenda will vary, depending upon the focus and the goals of the group, but normally include both routine items and some current issues or special projects. Minutes of the meeting should be taken and copies supplied to any members not in attendance, the managing partner (or executive committee), and the firm's administrator. See Appendix Y for a relatively simple Practice Group Meeting Agenda and Appendix Z for a more advanced Practice Group Meeting Agenda.

Preparing for Succession 19

Succession planning enables a firm to endure beyond the participation of its current leaders and business generators. Firms that have survived beyond their first generation of lawyers have experienced succession issues and have met the challenge of creating an institutional firm; that is, a firm with an existence and an identity that goes beyond that of the individual lawyers.

While most firms that have been around fifty years or more can improve on their succession planning, they must have developed some plan to survive the departure of the firm's founders and original leaders. Those firms have survived the transition crisis that commonly occurs when the founder and first-generation leaders leave the practice of law due to retirement, disability, or death.

Ironically, the stronger and more successful the original leaders of the firm, the more unprepared the others are to take over when the time comes. The transition from the first generation lawyers to the second generation is the most critical point in the survival of any law firm. Some lawyers have had years, if not decades, benefiting from working in a growing law firm managed by the firm's founder. In this circumstance, the next generation of lawyers is frequently ill prepared to assume a leadership role. In some cases, the problem is compounded by the fact that the founder is also the lead rainmaker. The demise of firms at this point in their evolution is not uncommon.

First-generation firms need a succession plan. Don't become the typical firm that waits until its senior members of the firm are in their sixties, only to be surprised to find out that it is too late to develop a successful transition plan. A workable transition plan takes a good ten years to orchestrate, at a minimum. For those firms that have struggled though one or more transitions, consider developing a more formal succession plan that will allow for seamless adjustment.

Step 1: Evaluate the Partnership Structure

Let's start with an assessment of your present circumstances. The first question to ask is whether the next generation of firm lawyers is adequately prepared to take over when the senior leaders reach retirement age. If not, why not? Is there a vacancy at the mid-level partner range? Or do you have lawyers at mid-level who are ill-suited or unprepared for a leadership position? A good succession plan contemplates a growing partnership with partners at all levels.

Next, look at the partnership structure. Does your partnership agreement contemplate the addition of new partners? Does your firm offer its valuable associates partnership opportunities? If so, do the associates know the criteria and the timeline for partnership? If the answer to any of these questions is "no," you will want to reevaluate your policies and procedures.

Is the firm a collection of individual practitioners or does it have a more unified institutional culture? Firms of five, ten or fifteen lawyers may be nothing more than a collection of individuals operating under the same roof. In those cases, the firm has no overriding identity and the individual lawyers are focused on their individual practices, not the overall success of the firm.

Step 2: Plan for the Growth and Evolution of the Firm

Have the lawyers come together and created a vision for the future, or a common purpose going forward? Or, are the lawyers simply in a reactive mode? If there is no vision or business plan for going forward, take a weekend and conduct a retreat devoted to that topic. With each passing year, competition makes it more difficult for firms to succeed without strategic planning at some level.

Conventional wisdom says that firms with fewer than ten lawyers will not grow, absent a decision and effort by the partners to grow. Firms of more than ten lawyers grow naturally, unless there is a decision to not grow.

The point to be made, however, is that if the firm wants to grow or not, it needs to focus on succession planning if its goal is to succeed beyond the participation of the present lawyers.

Step 3: Plan for Partners at Different Levels

Generation skipping may make sense as an estate planning tool, but not as a strategy for the law firm's successful evolution. Whether the firm is large or small, its enduring success will depend on the development of associates into partners, and new partners into mid-level partners.

Unless the firm makes a conscious effort to develop young lawyers along a career track within the firm, the natural result may be vacancies in the mid-level partner range, which means there are no candidates available for taking over leadership roles.

To plan for partners at different levels, the firm should have:

- A recruiting policy that provides for hiring associates at specific intervals
- An associate training and mentoring program designed to first help associates become good lawyers, and then teach them about marketing and client development, and finally introduce them to law firm management, allowing them to have some role or committee assignment
- A process of assisting associates in developing career plans
- A clear message to associates regarding the firm's partnership opportunities and a clear statement of the partnership criteria
- A formal associate evaluation program, at least annually, that provides associates with an evaluation of their progress

Many smaller firms do not provide their associates with good training, annual evaluations, nor a clear message about partnership. These firms suffer from costly associate turnover and are the ones that end up with vacancies in the partnership ranks.

Step 4: Provide Management Training

The associate will focus on learning how to practice law during the first year or two. Then there will be training on marketing and client development. Once an associate has successfully gotten on track as a practicing lawyer, consider the following:

- Expose the associate to the firm's expense budget and revenue needs, with a focus on understanding the effects of billable hours, hourly rates, realization, write-downs, write-offs, etc. Then make sure the associate appreciates how poor client in-take or failed client expectations affect the firm's bottom line. Some firms provide full financial disclosure to associates, while others choose to selectively package the financial data provided to keep some information confidential.

- Provide training sessions in which the associate learns how the firm is governed and the efforts expended by managers and leaders of the firm.

- Introduce associates to the management process by including them on certain committees responsible for certain management functions. Their performance on these committees will assist in identifying future leaders of the firm.

Identifying future leaders and training them in firm management matters is critical. Don't lose sight that the partners who understand firm management, particularly the financial aspects, will make better partners, regardless of whether they serve in a leadership or management role.

Step 5: Develop a Client Transitioning Plan

To avoid losing a client to another firm during the transition in leadership, there must be a well focused plan in place. Consider the following:

- There needs to be an active plan to expose every significant client to more than one lawyer within the firm. This could involve a second person on the file who is available to stand in for the primary lawyer, or it could be a lawyer from a different practice area who serves other aspects of the client's legal needs.

- Any efforts to stay in touch with the client (lunches, visits, etc.) should include the designated second lawyer.

- When the primary lawyer approaches retirement age, initiate a program for transitioning most of the work and the responsibility to the lawyer designated to take over the account. This needs to be conducted with sensitivity to the client's desire for a continuing role of the primary lawyer.

Make sure that the firm's compensation system encourages elder lawyers to transition their clients to other lawyers. If your system penalizes lawyers who transition clients to others, it will never happen.

Step 6: Create Positive Incentives for Seniors

Senior lawyers can be reluctant to transition their clients to others. A common excuse is: "My clients want only me and we would lose them if I get other lawyers involved." While there might be enough truth to that statement to have it warrant consideration in the planning process, the more likely reason for reluctance has to do with the firm's compensation plan. If successful in transitioning clients to others, how will that affect the senior partner's compensation? Whether the compensation system is formulistic or subjective, it is likely driven by productivity and without protection for the senior partner who transfers clients to others.

Transitioning clients is not as easy as it sounds. While the clients may have intense loyalty to one lawyer, it is likely that they have friendships or acquaintances with other highly respected lawyers in the community. The senior lawyer's departure from the firm presents the excuse for changing to an acquaintance in a different firm. Under all of the circumstances, transitioning to other lawyers within the firm can be a delicate and challenging goal. However difficult the process may be, it is better than doing nothing and seeing what happens when the senior partner leaves the firm.

Appendix A: Model Partnership Agreement—Long Form

PARTNERSHIP AGREEMENT

OF

_____

This Partnership Agreement of _____ is entered into and shall be effective as of the _____ day of _____, _____, by and among the parties hereto with the purpose of forming a general partnership pursuant to the provisions of the Uniform Partnership Act of the State of _____, on the following terms and conditions:

Article I
The Partnership

1.01 *Purposes*. The purpose of the Partnership is to engage in the practice of law, and activities incidental thereto, in the State of _____.

1.02 *Name*. The name of the Partnership (sometimes called "the Firm") shall be "_____." All business of the Partnership shall be conducted solely under that name. Unless it is deemed to be a violation of the Code of Professional Responsibility, the Partnership, at its election, shall have the continuing right to use as part of its name the surname of any deceased or retired Partner.

1.03 *Term*. This Agreement shall continue until dissolved under its terms. The Partnership shall not be dissolved by the admission of additional Partners or by the death, disability, retirement, expulsion or withdrawal of any Partner.

1.04 *Location.* The principal place of business of the Partnership shall be
_____, unless otherwise agreed by the
Partners. The Partnership may establish and maintain additional offices at
other locations approved by the Partners.

1.05 *Title to Property.* All real and personal property shall be owned by the
Partnership as an entity. No Partner shall have any ownership interest in the
Partnership property in his or her own individual name or right. Each Partner's
interest in the Partnership shall be personal property for all purposes.

1.06 *Prior Agreements.* All previous agreements, understandings and under-
takings, whether oral or written, among any Partners with respect to their association for the practice of law are hereby superseded in their entirety by this
Agreement.

Article II
The Partners

2.01 *Identification of Partners.* The Partners shall be the signatories to this
Agreement and such additional lawyers as the Partners shall from time to time
elect.

2.02 Outside Activities. No Partner shall act as an officer, director, general
partner or employee of any corporation, partnership, unincorporated association or other entity, or accept any public office or office in any political party,
or invest with any client, without the approval of the Partners.

2.03 *Disposition of Partners' Earned Income.* Each Partner shall pay into the
Firm all income received for law work, court appointments, lecturing or teaching, professional writing or editing, all commissions received as executor, administrator, trustee or guardian, all directors' fees and, unless determined otherwise by the Partners, all income received for holding public office.

2.04 *Admission of New Partners.* New Partners may be admitted from time to
time by vote of the Partners, as provided in Section 2.05:

(A) A new Partner shall become a party to this Agreement by signing an Addendum.

(B) Within twenty (20) days after any individual becomes a Partner or a
Partner marries, the Partner's spouse shall execute a consent form in-
dicating acceptance of this Agreement.

(C) A newly admitted Partner shall share, in accordance with this Agreement and his or her Partnership status, in the assets as well as the
debts, obligations and liabilities of the Partnership as of his or her effective date of admission.

2.05 *Management.* The management of the Firm shall be vested in the Partners, who may delegate responsibilities to an Executive Committee or a Managing Partner, except for the following decision powers, which are expressly reserved to the Partners under Section 2.06:

(A) Admission of new partners (supermajority vote required), as provided
in Section 2.04;

(B) Allocation of the capital requirements and the allocation and distributions of the profits, as provided in Sections 3.01, 3.03, and 3.04;

(C) Adjustments in the amount of capital;

(D) Creation or expansion of debt;

(E) Purchase and sale of real estate;

(F) Acquisition of new or additional space;

(G) Establishment of branch offices;

(H) Any approvals requested or required under Section 2.02 or 2.03 of this Agreement, pertaining to outside activities and disposition of earned income;

(I) Expulsion of or disability determination of any Partner, as provided by Sections 5.01, 5.03, 7.01, and 7.02;

(J) Extension of mandatory retirement dates or employment of retired Partners, under Sections 4.02 and 4.03;

(K) Amount of professional liability insurance maintained;

(L) Mergers with or into other law firms (supermajority vote required); and

(M) Dissolution of the Partnership.

2.06 *Voting.* Each Partner shall be entitled to one:

(1) vote. All issues shall be determined by a majority vote, except those designated as requiring a supermajority, which will require a _____ percent (__%) vote, and as otherwise required in Sections 5.03 and 7.02.

2.07 *Special Meetings.* Regular meetings of the Partnership shall be held no less frequently than quarterly. Special Partnership meetings may be called at any time by any _____ (__) or more of the Partners.

Article III
Capital, Distributions and Allocation of Profit

3.01 *Contributions.* Each Partner shall be required to contribute money or other property to the Partnership in accordance with policies established by the Partners.

3.02 *Capital Account.* An individual capital account shall be established and maintained for each Partner in accordance with the provisions of the Internal Revenue Code. Each Partner's capital account (a) shall be increased by (i) the amount of money and fair market value of property contributed to the Partnership and (ii) the Partner's allocable share of income and gain allocated pursuant to this Agreement, and (b) shall be decreased by (i) the amount of money and fair market value of property distributed to that Partner and (ii) that Partner's allocable share of deductions and loss allocated pursuant to this Agreement. No Partner shall have a deficit capital account at the end of any Partnership year.

3.03 *Allocations.* Except as may be required by the Internal Revenue Code, all items of income, gain, deduction, loss and credit shall be allocated among the Partners for each Partnership year, in accordance with policies established by the Partners.

3.04 *Distributions.* Distribution of Partnership cash will be made periodically, in accordance with the policies established by the Partners.

Article IV
Retirement of Partners

4.01 *Voluntary Retirement.* A Partner may elect to retire from the Partnership by giving _____ (__) days written notice delivered to the Partners. A Partner shall be deemed "Retired" under the terms of this Agreement only if, in addition to the foregoing, the Partner no longer engages in the practice of law.

4.02 *Mandatory Retirement.* Effective as of the end of the year in which a Partner attains the age of _____ (__), the Partner shall enter retirement status unless the Partners by a majority vote at the written request of the Partner affected extends the inception date of such status to a later date, in which case it may further extend such date from time to time. No extension shall be for more than one (1) year.

4.03 *Employment of Retired Partners.* Subject to approval of the Partnership by appropriate vote, the employment of any Retired Partner by the Partnership may be established on a full or part-time basis, on terms mutually acceptable, but in no event for single periods exceeding one (1) year.

4.04 *Amounts to Be Paid upon Retirement of a Partner.* The Partnership shall acquire the interest of a retired Partner by paying:

(A) An amount equal to the credit balance, if any, of the Partner's capital account; plus

(B) An amount equal to the undistributed share of the profits of such Partner for the year during which the retirement occurred, attributable to the interest in profits of such Partner from the beginning of such year to the close of the month during which the retirement occurred.

Article V
Disability of a Partner

5.01 *Temporary Disability.* A Partner shall be temporarily disabled when the Partners, by affirmative vote of at least _____ percent (___%) of the Partners (exclusive of the Partner affected), determine that he or she is temporarily unable to adequately engage in the practice of law due to any physical or mental condition.

5.02 *Payments to Temporarily Disabled Partners.* From the date of determination of temporary disability, a disabled Partner shall be paid by the Firm, in lieu of any other distribution or profits, the following:

(A) For the first _____ (__) months, his or her monthly draw and, when such distribution is made to all Partners generally, his or her share of the Firm's net profits for such period; and

(B) For the next _____ (__) months, ___ % of the amount specified in Section 5.02(A).

Full resumption of responsibility for Partnership duties shall be determined by the Partners, as required in Section 5.01, and shall result in termination of the foregoing payments.

5.03 *Permanent Disability.* A Partner shall be considered permanently disabled when the Partners, by the affirmative vote of at least _____ percent

(___%) of the Partners (exclusive of the Partner affected), determine that he or she is permanently unable to adequately engage in the practice of law due to any physical or mental condition. A Partner shall be considered permanently disabled after _____ (_) months of temporary disability.

5.04 *Payments to Permanently Disabled Partners.* A determination of permanent disability of a Partner will terminate his or her rights as a Partner in the Firm. The Partner shall be considered retired as of the date of the permanent disability determination and will receive payments as set forth in Section 4.04.

5.05 *Medical Exam.* If there is any reasonable doubt as to whether a Partner is disabled, the Partner shall submit to an examination, at the Partnership's expense, by an appropriate physician selected by the Partnership. The physician's opinion shall be considered by the Partners.

Article VI
Death of a Partner

6.01 *Death.* Upon the death of a Partner, the interest of the deceased Partner shall be terminated as of the end of the month following the date of death.

6.02 *Amounts to Be Paid upon the Death of a Partner.* The Partnership shall acquire the interest of a deceased Partner by paying to his or her estate or personal representative all the proceeds of any life insurance maintained by the Partnership on the life of that Partner for the benefit of his or her Estate (and other than any life insurance maintained by the Partnership for the sole benefit of the Firm), but in no event less than an amount equal to the credit balance, if any, of the Partner's capital account. Such capital account shall be adjusted for each Partner's share of income, gain, deductions and loss for the year during which the death occurred, attributable to the interest of such Partner from the beginning of such year to the close of the month during which the death occurred.

Article VII
Withdrawal or Expulsion of Partner

7.01 *Withdrawal.* Any Partner may voluntarily withdraw from the Firm at the end of any calendar month, upon three (3) months written notice to the Partners, who shall be entitled to accelerate the effective date of the withdrawal by a vote of the majority.

7.02 *Expulsion.* The Partners, by appropriate secret ballot vote of at least _____ percent (___%) of the Partners (excluding therefrom the vote of the Partner whose expulsion is under consideration), may expel any Partner without notice. Without limiting the foregoing, Partners have agreed that any of the following are unacceptable to the Firm and, unless otherwise determined by the Partners, there will likely be a vote of expulsion if such Partner:

(A) Is disbarred, suspended or is the subject of other major disciplinary action of any duly constituted authority;

(B) Engages in professional misconduct or violates the Rules of Professional Conduct;

(C) Engages in any action that injures the professional standing of the Partnership, if such action continues after desistance has been requested by the Firm;

(D) Is declared insolvent or bankrupt or makes an assignment of assets for the benefit of his or her creditors;

(E) Breaches any provision of this Agreement which the Partnership deems a major provision, if, after such breach has been specified as a prospective ground for expulsion by written notice given by the Partnership, the same breach continues or occurs again;

(F) Habitually lacks attention to the business of the Partnership and to the interests of the clients of the Partnership and if, after notice of such conduct from the Partnership, he or she continues to so act;

(G) Fails to file any state or federal tax return or if any federal or state authority determines that such Partner has committed an act of tax evasion; or

(H) Commits an act of willful misconduct or gross negligence resulting in a loss to the Partnership, whether or not such act is the subject of a claim against the professional liability insurance of the Partnership.

7.03 *Client Letter*. The Announcement to clients regarding the withdrawing/expelled Partner's departure from the Partnership shall be sent within _____ (__) days of the notice of withdrawal to clients for which the withdrawing/expelled Partner had been designated as the originating, responsible or billing attorney. The announcement shall be made by letter in a manner acceptable to the Firm. During the notice period, and until the client letter is mailed, the withdrawing/expelled Partner shall not contact, solicit or send announcements to any clients regarding such withdrawal/expulsion. Nothing herein shall be deemed to interfere with the right of all clients to select their own counsel.

7.04 *Disposition of Client Files*. If a withdrawing/expelled Partner intends to continue the private practice of law, the Partnership shall notify each of the withdrawing/expelled Partner's clients in accordance with Section 7.03:

(A) All files, documents and records of the withdrawing/expelled Partner's clients shall, unless otherwise directed by the client, remain in the possession of the Partnership, but such former Partner shall have access to such files, documents and records in existence at the Partner's departure date, for purposes of inspection and/or copying at any time during business hours, without cost or obligation on the part of the Partnership.

(B) Only upon the written request of the client shall the files, documents and records of that client be delivered to a withdrawing/expelled Partner, in which event such former Partner shall be obligated thereafter to make such files, documents and records freely available to the Partnership during business hours.

7.05 *Allocation of Fees and Expenses between Firm and Withdrawing/Expelled Partner*. Revenues to be received for uncompleted matters for clients retained by a withdrawing/expelled Partner shall be allocated between the Partnership and the departing Partner as follows:

(A) Any payments received by the withdrawing/expelled Partner shall first be allocated to the Partnership to satisfy the client's outstanding receivables existing as of the Partner's withdrawal/expulsion date or later billed by the Partnership for services or expenses incurred prior to the Partner's departure;

(B) As to any contingent fee clients retained by the withdrawing/expelled Partner, the fee ultimately earned shall be divided between the Partnership and the withdrawing/expelled Partner based on the relative amount of effort expended; and

(C) Prior to the allocation of any revenues, costs or other expenses incurred shall be reimbursed first to the Partnership and then to the withdrawing/expelled Partner.

7.06 Amounts to Be Paid to a Withdrawing/Expelled Partner. The Partnership shall acquire the interest of a withdrawing/expelled Partner by paying:

(A) An amount equal to the credit balance, if any, of the Partner's capital account; plus

(B) An amount equal to the undistributed share of the profits of such Partner for the year during which the withdrawal/expulsion occurred, attributable to the interest in profits of such Partner from the beginning of such year to the close of the month during which the withdrawal/expulsion occurred.

7.07 *Indemnification*. Effective as of the date that the Firm shall receive written notice from a client of the selection of the withdrawing/expelled Partner as its counsel, the withdrawing/expelled Partner to whom the matter has been allocated shall be responsible for the services to be provided to the client, and he or she shall be deemed to indemnify the Partnership and hold it harmless against any claims asserted against the Partnership by reason of any event or act relating to said matters which occurred subsequent to the date of selection.

Article VIII
Payment Obligations and Related Matters

8.01 *Time of Payment*. Subject to the calculations applicable under Article 7.05(C) and the limitations contained in Section 8.02, the amounts due a partner entitled to payment herein shall be paid as follows: capital accounts shall be paid in _____ (___) equal monthly payments commencing within ____ (___) days of the departure date, unless restricted by the percentage limitation set forth in Section 8.02. The term "departure date" as used herein shall mean the date a Partner's interest in the Partnership is terminated under the terms of this Agreement.

8.02 *Limits on Payment Obligations*. Notwithstanding anything contained elsewhere herein to the contrary:

(A) Any negative balance of a departed Partner's capital account shall be fully and immediately due and payable by that Partner, and it shall be paid or offset, as the case may be, before any payments which otherwise may be owing to the departed Partner are paid.

(B) If at any Partnership meeting the public accountants compiling the financial reports and statements of the Partnership report that the total payments being made under Sections 6.02 and 7.06 have exceeded, for any month during the prior three months, a sum in excess of an amount equal to _____ percent (__%) of the average monthly net income of the Partnership (as computed under the method of accounting used by the Partnership) during the three months immediately preceding the later three months, then the Partners may, at their sole discretion, reduce all periodic payments being or to be made to departed Partners and extend the time of payment of all sums to be paid under this Article proportionately, so as to reduce the total of all such payments during the following quarter to a total monthly amount which is not more than that said _____ percent (__%) of the average monthly net income of the Partnership during such prior six months.

(C) Except with respect to a deceased Partner or disabled Partner and notwithstanding the other provisions of this Agreement, if an election to dissolve the Partnership should be made within not more than ninety (90) days after a Partner's departure date, such Partner shall not receive, and the Partnership shall not be required to make, any of the payments called for by the other Sections of this Article; such Partner shall have such rights, obligations, duties, powers and privileges as though such Partner's departure date had not occurred.

(D) No interest shall be paid on any unpaid balance due either by or to the Partnership to or from a retiring, withdrawing or expelled Partner under this Agreement, except that if a payment is not made when due (unless such payments are excused, extended or reduced under subparagraph (B) above), it shall thereafter bear interest at the rate of interest of one percent (1%) over the Prime Rate of interest then charged by the _____.

(E) The payment of any sum by the Partnership under Section 6.02 or 7.06 shall be deemed to be payment in full for the departed Partner's interest in all of the assets of the Partnership, tangible or otherwise.

8.03 *No Goodwill.* The omission of any provision in this Agreement for the valuation of Partnership goodwill is deliberate. There is no goodwill in connection with the business of this Partnership, and no Partner shall have the right to receive payment for his or her interest in the alleged goodwill of the Partnership.

Article IX
Professional Liability

9.01 *Insurance Coverage.* The Partnership shall maintain professional liability insurance coverage for all, in such amounts as the Partners may from time to time determine.

Article X
Dissolution

10.01 *Election to Dissolve.* The Partnership may be dissolved at any time by a vote of _____ percent (__%) of the Partners at a meeting called expressly to consider dissolution. Upon the enactment of a Resolution to Dissolve, no further professional services shall be rendered in the Partnership name, and no further business shall be transacted from and after the date selected for dissolution except to the extent necessary to wind up the affairs of the Partnership. Maintenance of offices to effectuate the winding up or liquidation of the Partnership affairs shall not be construed as a continuation of the Partnership.

10.02 *Duty of Partner.* Notwithstanding the foregoing, in the event of dissolution each Partner owes a duty to the Partnership and its clients to complete all unfinished work, and each Partner selected by a client to continue such work shall hold the other Partners and the Partnership harmless in that regard. In addition:

(A) Each Partner warrants and represents that he or she shall not at any time aid, abet, assist or encourage a client or any other third party in litigation between a client of the Partnership on one hand, and the Partnership on the other hand, concerning work performed by the Partnership for the client, including but not limited to the client's obligation to pay the Partnership for services rendered to the client on the client's behalf. Nothing contained herein is intended to or shall be construed to interfere with or violate existing statute or case authority requiring persons to comply with subpoenas duly issued and properly served.

(B) All Partners covenant to cooperate in every regard in the winding up of the Partnership affairs and, without limiting the generality of the foregoing, will refrain from the following conduct:
(1) Transferring Partnership assets;
(2) Failing to comply with client directives to turn over client files;
(3) Refusing to sign substitutions of attorney forms on behalf of the Firm;
(4) Removing client files from the offices of the Partnership without noting on a permanent log that is available for inspection by any party or counsel;
(5) Refusing any other Partners access to the Firm offices;
(6) Removing any Partnership books of account of records;
(7) Refusing access to personal effects, office forms, files, word processing disks and word processing equipment; and
(8) Tampering with information found in computers and files used by the Firm or any member of the Partnership.

(C) Upon dissolution, any Partner remaining in the space occupied by the Partnership shall pay to the Partnership the fair market rental value for the rent of that space until such time as he or she shall remove himself or herself from the premises.

(D) Each Partner shall be allowed to purchase the furniture in his or her office at an evaluation set by the appraiser who appraises all the other office furniture in the suite for purposes of sale and liquidation.

10.03 *Disposition of Client Files.* In the event of dissolution of the Partnership, all files, documents and records pertaining to each client shall be delivered to the appropriate Partners, subject to any written desire of any client.

10.04 *Costs of Liquidation.* The Partnership assets shall be used to pay or provide for all debts of the Partnership and all costs of liquidation.

10.05 *Distribution to Partners.* After payment of the debts of the Partnership and the costs of liquidation, the remaining assets shall, upon dissolution and liquidation of the Partnership, be allocated among the Partners in the following order:

(A) In payment of loans to or for the benefit of the Partnership; and

(B) To the Partners in accordance with their credit balance, if any, of their capital account, after giving effect to all contributions, distributions and allocations for all periods. Any indebtedness of any Partner to the Partnership as of the date of dissolution of the Partnership shall be deducted from each distribution to which he or she may otherwise be entitled pursuant to this Section, to the extent required to satisfy and discharge such indebtedness.

10.06 *Waiver of Right to Court Decree of Dissolution.* The Partners agree that irreparable damage would be done to the relationships between Partners and clients and to the reputation of the Partnership if any Partner should bring an action in court to dissolve this Partnership. Care has been taken in this Partnership Agreement to provide fair and just payments to be made to a Partner whose relationship with the Partnership is terminated for any reason. Accordingly, each of the Partners accepts the provisions under this Partnership Agreement as the Partner's sole entitlement on termination of the Partnership relationship. Each Partner hereby waives and renounces his or her right to seek an independent adversarial appointment by a court of a liquidator or receiver for the Partnership, but each does agree to resolve all matters, including, if necessary, by use of the procedure set forth in Article XI below.

Article XI
Arbitration

11.01 *Arbitration.* Except with respect to controversies as to the compensation of Partners, which are to be determined solely in accordance with the terms of this Agreement, any controversy arising out of or relating to this Agreement or to the enforcement of this Agreement shall be settled by arbitration in accordance with the rules of the American Arbitration Association then in effect, provided, however, that the Board of Arbitrators shall consist of not more than three persons selected by the parties in controversy, and provided, however, if the parties cannot agree on the selection of such Arbitrators, that _____. Judgment upon any arbitration award rendered in accordance herewith may be entered in any court having jurisdiction thereof.

Article XII
General Provisions

12.01 *Complete Agreement and Amendments.* This Partnership Agreement constitutes the entire agreement between the Partners and supersedes all prior agreements, representations, warranties, statements, promises and understandings (whether oral or written) with respect to the subject matter hereof. This Agreement may not be amended, altered or modified except by a writing executed by _____ percent (___%) of the Partners, which writing makes specific reference to this Agreement and the intent of the Partners to amend this Agreement.

12.02 *Books, Records and Accounting, Fiscal Year.* The Partnership's books and records, together with all of the documents and papers pertaining to the business of the Partnership, shall be kept at the principal place of business of the Partnership, and at all reasonable times shall be open to the inspection of, and may be copied and excerpts taken therefrom by, any Partner or his or her duly authorized representative. The books and records of the Partnership shall be kept on a calendar-year basis in accordance with the cash method of accounting required for federal income tax purposes, consistently applied, and shall reflect all Partnership transactions and be appropriate and adequate for the Partnership business.

12.03 *Notices.* All notices under this Agreement shall be in writing and shall be served upon the other parties at the addresses set forth in the books and records of the Partnership.

12.04 *Severability.* If any provision of this Agreement shall be found by a court of competent jurisdiction to be illegal, in conflict with any law of the State of _____ or otherwise unenforceable, the validity and enforceability of the remaining provisions shall not be affected, and the rights and obligations of the parties shall be construed and enforced as if this Agreement did not contain the particular provision found to be illegal, invalid or otherwise unenforceable.

12.05 *Survival of Rights.* Except as provided herein to the contrary, this Partnership Agreement shall be binding upon and inure to the benefit of the parties signatory hereto (as well as to all future parties who are admitted as Partners in this Partnership), their respective spouses, heirs, executors, legal representatives and permitted successors and assigns.

12.06 *Waiver.* No consent or waiver, express or implied by a Partner or the Partnership, to the breach or default by any Partner in the performance of his or her obligations under this Agreement shall be deemed or construed to be a consent or waiver to any other breach or default.

12.07 *Further Assurances.* Each party hereto agrees to do all acts and things and to make, execute and deliver such written instruments as shall from time to time be reasonably required to carry out the terms and provisions of this Partnership Agreement.

[SIGNATURE]

[SIGNATURE]

[SIGNATURE]

[SIGNATURE]

[SIGNATURE]

Appendix B:
Model Partnership
Agreement—Short Form

This Partnership Agreement is entered into this _____ day of _____ 200_ by and between _____, _____, _____, _____, _____ and _____. The parties mutually covenant and agree as follows:

Article I
Name, Purpose, Location

1.1 The parties will carry on in partnership under the name of _____, herein sometimes referred to as "the Firm."

1.2 The purpose of the partnership will be the practice of law.

1.3 The principal place of business shall be _____ _____.

Article II
Partners

2.1 The Partners are _____, _____, _____, _____, _____, _____, _____ and _____ and such other lawyers as may be offered an invitation to join the Partnership in the future as Partners in accordance with Article 2.3 and accept the terms of this Agreement by signing an Addendum.

2.2 In matters requiring a vote of the Partnership, each Partner shall have one equal vote.

2.3 A simple majority vote of Partners shall govern unless otherwise provided in Article 2.3. Voting by proxy is not allowed.

2.4 A supermajority vote of 80% of those eligible to vote is required for the following actions:
- Making an offer of partnership to another lawyer;
- Requiring a capital contribution from existing or future Partners;
- Amending this Partnership Agreement;
- Establishing or amending the Partner compensation system;
- Creating or expanding credit lines or incurring debt in excess of $_____;
- Purchasing or selling real estate;
- Establishing a branch office;
- Merging with another law firm;
- Making a disability determination under Article VII; or
- Expelling a Partner under Article IX.

2.5 All revenue received by each Partner from the practice of law shall be paid over to the Partnership and all revenue from activities related to the practice of law shall be disclosed to all other Partners and subject to a determination of the Partners as to whether it is to be treated as Partnership revenue.

2.6 No Partner may engage in the practice of law under any other firm name or in any other capacity.

Article III
Capital

3.1 The capital of the Firm shall consist of the initial contributions made by the Partners as set forth on attached Exhibit A and such other contributions as determined by the Firm from time to time to enable it to conduct its business.

3.2 No interest shall be paid on the Partner's capital accounts.

Article IV
Partner Compensation

4.1 Distribution of compensation to Partners shall be in accordance with policies as from time to time established by the Partners.

4.2 Drawing accounts shall be created for each Partner and the Partner's share of profit or losses shall be credited or charged to his or her drawing account. No interest shall be paid or charged on credit or debit balances of any drawing account.

Article V
Management

5.1 The management of the firm shall be vested in the Partners, who may delegate responsibilities to a Managing Partner, with the exception of the actions set forth in Article 2.3, which cannot be delegated and which are subject to a supermajority vote of the Partners.

Article VI
Retirement of Partners

6.1 A Partner may elect to retire from the Partnership by giving 60 days written notice to the Partners. A Partner shall be deemed retired under this agreement only if, in addition to the foregoing, the Partner no longer engages in the practice of law.

6.2 The Partnership may acquire the interest of a retired Partner by paying or charging the Partner:

A. An amount equal to the credit or debit balance, if any, in the partner's capital account as of the date of retirement; and

B. An amount equal to the credit or debit balance, if any, in the Partner's drawing account as of the date of retirement.

Article VII
Disability of Partners

7.1 A Partner shall be deemed temporarily disabled when the Partners, by affirmative vote in accordance with Article II, determine that he or she is temporarily unable to engage in the practice of law due to any physical or mental condition. A temporarily disabled partner's right to continued compensation shall be limited to his or her regular compensation for a period of 60 days. Beyond the 60 days of continuing compensation set forth herein, the Partners agree that they will each rely on disability insurance to protect themselves from the financial needs while disabled.

7.2 A Partner shall be considered permanently disabled when the Partners, by affirmative vote in accordance with Article II, determine that he or she is permanently unable to engage in the practice of law due to any physical or mental condition. A permanently disabled partner's right to continued compensation shall be limited to his or her regular compensation for a period of 60 days.

7.3 The partnership shall acquire the interest of a permanently disabled partner by paying:

A. An amount equal to the credit balance, if any, on the partner's capital account; and

B. An amount equal to the credit balance, if any, on the partner's drawing account.

7.4 The firm shall have no further responsibility for payments to temporarily or permanently disabled Partners, with the understanding that disability insurance is available to be purchased by the firm or by the individual to cover the situation.

Article VIII
Death of a Partner

8.1 Upon the death of a Partner, the interest of the deceased Partner shall be terminated as of the date of death.

8.2 The partnership shall acquire the interest of a deceased partner by paying to his or her estate:

A. An amount equal to the credit balance, if any, on the partner's capital account; and

B. An amount equal to the credit balance, if any, on the partner's drawing account.

Article IX
Withdrawal or Expulsion of a Class A Partner

9.1 Any Partner may voluntarily withdraw from the Firm at the end of any calendar month, upon three months written notice to the Partners, who shall be entitled to accelerate the date of withdrawal by a vote of the majority.

9.2 The Partners, by appropriate secret vote ballot, may expel any Partner without notice. Without limiting the foregoing, Partners have agreed that any of the following are unacceptable to the Firm and, unless otherwise determined by the Partners, there will likely be a vote of expulsion if the Partner:

    A. Is disbarred, suspended or is the subject of other major disciplinary action of any duly constituted authority;

    B. Engages in any action that injures the professional standing of the Partnership, if such action continues after desistance has been requested by the Firm;

    C. Refuses to abide by the provision of the Partnership Agreement; or

    D. Habitually lacks attention to the business of the Partnership or to the interests of the clients of the Partnership and if, after notice from the Partnership, he or she continues to so act.

9.3 The announcement to clients regarding the withdrawing/expelled Partner's departure from the Partnership shall be sent to those clients for whom the withdrawing/expelled Partner has been designated as the responsible (billing) lawyer. The announcement shall be made by letter in a manner acceptable to the Firm and signed by both the departing/expelled Partner and the Firm. Until the announcement is mailed, the withdrawing/expelled Partner shall not contact, solicit or send announcements to any clients regarding such withdrawal/expulsion.

9.4 All files of the withdrawing/expelled Partner shall, unless otherwise directed by the client, remain in the possession of the Partnership.

9.5 Nothing herein shall be deemed to interfere with the right of all clients to select their own counsel.

9.6 Following the departure, revenues received by the withdrawing/expelled Partner from any client shall first be allocated to any unpaid fees and unreimbursed expenses of _____ before being applied to any new work performed by the departed partner.

9.7 The Partnership shall acquire the interest of the withdrawing/expelled Partner by paying:

    A. An amount equal to the credit balance, if any, on the Partner's capital account; and

    B. An amount equal to the credit balance, if any, on the Partner's drawing account.

Article X
Professional Liability Insurance

10.1 The Partnership shall maintain professional liability insurance for all lawyers, in such amounts as the Partners may from time to time determine.

Article XI
Dissolution

11.1 The Partnership may be dissolved by a vote of 80% of the Partners at a meeting called expressly to consider dissolution.

11.2 Notwithstanding the foregoing, in the event of dissolution each Partner owes a duty to the Partnership and its clients to complete all unfinished work, and each Partner selected by a client to continue such work shall hold the other Partners and the Partnership harmless in that regard.

11.3 All Partners covenant to cooperate in every regard in the winding up of the Partnership affairs.

11.4 The Partnership assets shall be used to pay or provide for all debts of the Partnership and all costs of liquidation.

11.5 After payment of the debts of the Partnership and the costs of liquidation, the remaining assets shall be allocated to the Partners with priority first given to loans made by the partners, then to payment of capital accounts, if any, and then finally to an equal distribution of the balance to the partners.

Article XII
Other Provisions

12.1 The official books of account of the Partnership will be maintained on a calendar year basis.

12.2 All provisions of this agreement shall be construed according to the laws of the State of _____.

12.3 If any portion of this agreement shall be held unenforceable, void or invalid, the remainder of the agreement shall be unaffected and shall nevertheless be carried into effect.

12.4 Any controversy or claim arising out of or relating to this Agreement, or breach thereof, shall be resolved by an arbitration process as determined by the Partners, but failing agreement on the process, in accordance with the rules and procedures of the American Arbitration Association.

IN WITNESS WHEREOF, the Partners have executed this Agreement at _____ on the day and year written above.

_____
[SIGNATURE]

_____
[SIGNATURE]

_____
[SIGNATURE]

_____
[SIGNATURE]

_____
[SIGNATURE]

Appendix C: The Management Committee: Role and Responsibilities

The Management Committee is responsible for the general management of the firm, with the exception of those matters that are specifically reserved for the Partners. The Committee is composed of the Managing Partner and two other Partners elected for staggered two year terms. The Legal Administrator supports and participates with the Management Committee as a non-voting member.

Management Committee Meetings are held from 8:30–9:30 a.m. each Friday morning. The Managing Partner, with the assistance of the Legal Administrator, prepares the agenda that is circulated to the other Committee Members in advance of each meeting. Minutes of the Management Committee Meetings are to be circulated to all Partners by the following Monday afternoon.

Partnership Meetings shall be held quarterly at 4:30 p.m. on the second Tuesday of January, April, July, and October of each year. The Managing Partner, with the assistance of the Legal Administrator, shall prepare an agenda that will be circulated to the Partners at least 48 hours prior to the meeting. The Managing Partner will preside at the Partnership meetings.

The responsibility of the Management Committee will be to:

- Direct the development of annual and long-term strategic business plans
- Oversee the Firm's initiative with the goal to maximize long-term profitability
- Administer the Firm's Partner Compensation Plan
- Assure the timely completion of the Firm's annual operating and capital budgets

- Maintain favorable banking relationships
- Establish and oversee the Firm policies for the management of timekeeping, billing, work-in-process, accounts receivables, and collections
- Assure a positive work environment calculated to maximize the productivity of partners, associates, paralegals and staff
- Enforce the Firm's policies and procedures
- Assure the firm is legally and ethically operated
- Oversee the hiring, training and evaluation of support staff and administrative staff
- Manage and oversee the evaluation process and the compensation plan for associates, paralegals and staff
- Oversee all building and leasehold matters

The Management Committee is authorized to delegate its responsibilities to other Partners, the Legal Administrator and/or other staff members.

Appendix D: Managing Partner Job Description

The Managing Partner shall have management responsibilities for the Law Firm, with the exception of those matters specifically reserved to the Partners in Section ___ of the Partnership Agreement. The Managing Partner shall serve the Firm in the following ways, subject to the right to delegate certain of the functions to the Firm's Administrator, Administrative Staff or a Committee:

1. Leadership
   a. Executing the long-term goals and objectives that have been established by the Partnership
   b. Assisting the Partnership in developing annual and long-term strategic plans
   c. Providing the leadership necessary to achieve the Firm's profitability needs and/or goals
   d. Communicating with the Firm Partners
   e. Directing the functions of the Firm's Administrator
   f. Acting as the voice of the Firm, internally and externally
   g. Interfacing with Firm members on all matters of importance
2. Meetings
   a. Setting the agendas for and chairing Partnership Meetings
   b. Creating agendas for and chairing meetings of the Management Committee, if applicable
   c. Coordinating and supporting the work of other Committees
3. Finance
   a. Developing an annual operating budget and capital budget
   b. Monitoring the budget on a monthly basis, overseeing spending to assure compliance with the limitations of the expense budget

    c. Tracking revenue and working with Practice Groups and individual lawyers to help achieve the revenue budget amount

    d. Insuring compliance with billing and collection policies

    e. Approving write-offs of work in process and receivables

    f. Overseeing the Partners' capital accounts and drawing accounts

    g. Managing banking relationships and monitoring the use of any line of credit

4. <u>Personnel</u>

    a. Overseeing the hiring and orientation of new staff

    b. Recommending staff benefits

    c. Overseeing evaluations, setting salaries, and assuring the professional development of staff

    d. Disciplining staff and handling terminations

    e. Overseeing compliance with the Firm's policies and procedures

    f. Creating and implementing new policies, as necessary

5. <u>Technology and Equipment</u>

    a. Managing the effective and efficient use of the Firm's technology by arranging for necessary training

    b. Providing lawyers and staff with computer support, necessary programs, etc.

    c. Learning about new technology, conducting cost/benefit analyses, and making purchase recommendations to the Partnership

    d. Having responsibility for equipment, including maintenance, repair and service contracts

6. <u>Building and Grounds</u>

    a. Overseeing the physical plant and the facilities

    b. Negotiating leases and related arrangements

7. <u>Practice Management</u>

    a. Providing information and support to the Practice Groups

    b. Coordinating the work of the Practice Groups

8. <u>Marketing</u>

    a. Coordinating the marketing efforts of Practice Groups and/or individual Lawyers

    b. Supervising the Firm's marketing efforts

9. <u>Miscellaneous</u>

    a. Directing the social agenda of the Firm

    b. Planning and coordinating Firm retreats

    c. Maintaining accessibility to lawyers, staff and clients

    d. Keeping up on trends in law firm management

Appendix E:
Legal Administrator
Small Firm

The Legal Administrator manages the business operations of the firm on a day-to-day basis, reporting directly to the Managing Partner. The specific responsibilities to be performed under the general guidance of the Managing Partner include:

1. Meeting with the Managing Partner on a regular basis to provide input and exchange information necessary to the management of the firm
2. Attending and participating in various firm meetings and committees as requested by the Managing Partner
3. Initiating, recommending and assuring adherence to all policies and procedures of the firm
4. Developing and implementing all office systems, including:
   a. Filing systems, electronic and hard copy
   b. Telephone and other systems
   c. Library setup and maintenance
5. Manage the firm's technology programs to insure the needs of the firm are met, including:
   a. Oversee the computer systems design to insure it meets the needs of the firm
   b. Perform cost/benefit analysis for potential purchases
   c. Work with outside vendors to insure an effective system is maintained
   d. Develop a forecast of revenues needed for the maintenance and the upgrade of computer systems, both hardware and software
   e. Be responsible for the maintenance of the telephone and other systems. If needed, review and recommend changes needed to insure firm needs are met

6. Managing and directing the human resources of the firm including recruiting, training, developing compensation and benefits, measuring performance, conducting annual evaluations and disciplining, as necessary
7. Assisting in budget development and other financial matters
8. Assisting in marketing efforts and public relations
9. Managing the building and business premises including all landlord tenant relationships. Responsibilities of the facilities management function include:
   a. Review office space regularly and compare to long range planning efforts to insure firm is positioned to meet future needs
   b. Make recommendations regarding space planning needs and manage the design of new, additional or renovation of space
   c. Manage lease negotiations, with direction from the Managing Partner
   d. Arrange for property insurance
   e. Manage and/or participate in other facilities management functions as determined by the managing partner

Appendix F:
Legal Administrator
Large Firm

The Legal Administrator is an employee of the firm who manages the business operations on a day-to-day basis, reporting to the Managing Partner (or Chair of the Management Committee). The responsibilities of the position include:

1. Attend and participate in various firm meetings and committees. Participate as a non-voting member of the Management Committee. Prepare the draft agenda and distribute prior to the meeting. Assure timely and accurate record keeping and distribution of minutes of all Management Committee meetings. Attend all partnership meetings as directed by the Managing Partner (or Chair of the Management Committee). Prepare and distribute the draft agenda prior to the meetings. Assure the timely and accurate record keeping and distribution of minutes of all firm meetings and decisions made by the partnership. Attend and participate such other meetings of committees or practice group as deemed appropriate.
2. Coordinate all business-planning efforts at the direction of the Managing Partner and/or Management Committee with the goal to maximize long-term profitability. Be responsible for developing and recommending long-range planning strategies. Research and review current trends in the legal profession to predict future firm planning needs and efforts.
3. Initiate and recommend administrative policies and assure adherence to approved firm policies. Be responsible for the development and implementation of all office systems, policies and procedures including:
   a. Technology programs and systems
   b. The Policy & Procedures Manual
   c. The library setup and maintenance

4. Manage and direct the human resources of the firm including recruiting, training, developing compensation and benefits, measuring performance, conducting annual evaluations and disciplining, as necessary. These responsibilities include:
   a. Coordinating and participating in the evaluation process of support and administrative staff
   b. Implementing the compensation plan and benefits, for firm support staff and administrative personnel
   c. Being responsible for the recruitment, orientation, training, discipline and termination of firm support staff and administrative personnel
   d. Being responsible for the development and implementation of job design and position descriptions
   e. Allocating human resources for the best utilization
   f. Insuring effective employee relations, acting as the point person for firm support staff and administrative personnel
   g. Establish procedures for, and then supervise, the maintenance of personnel files
5. Manage the firm's technology programs to insure hardware and software meet business requirements. Management of the technology program includes:
   a. Annually reviewing the current technology systems to insure full utilization of equipment and to insure equipment is up to date
   b. Overseeing the computer systems design to insure it meets the needs of the firm
   c. Performing cost/benefit analyses
   d. Working with outside vendors to insure an effective system is maintained
   e. Developing a forecast of revenues needed for the maintenance and the upgrade of computer systems, both hardware and software
   f. Being responsible for the maintenance and upgrade, if necessary, of the telephone system
6. Manage the building and business premises, including the landlord—tenant relationship and contracted services. Responsibilities of the facilities management function include:
   a. Reviewing office space regularly and comparing to long-range planning efforts to insure firm is positioned to meet future needs
   b. Making recommendations regarding space planning needs and managing the design of new, additional or renovation of space
   c. Managing lease negotiations, with direction from the Managing Partner and/or Management Committee
   d. Supervising purchasing of supplies and inventory control
   e. Managing and/or participating in other facilities management functions as determined by the firm
7. Assist practice groups and the partners with:
   a. Recruiting lawyer personnel
   b. Assisting with the implementation of the orientation and training of associate lawyers
   c. Implementing work product quality control systems

    d. Assisting in the development of, and adherence to, firm professional standards

    e. Managing other functions deemed appropriate by the Managing Partner and/or the Management Committee

8. Insure the client development/marketing activities of the firm are appropriate and beneficial to the firm's success. Responsibilities include:

    a. Performing profitability studies

    b. Identifying business opportunities

    c. Initiating and assisting with client development activities

    d. Acting as the public relations director of the firm, as needed, by interacting with outside sources to insure the firm has good visibility within its service area

The Legal Administrator has the authority to delegate any of the above responsibilities with the prior approval of the Managing Partner and/or the Management Committee.

Note: I would like to thank my partner Sandra J. Boyer from Boyer Greene L.L.C. for providing this Sample Legal Administrator Job Description, which relates to consulting work she performs assisting firms in recruiting, transitioning, and counseling legal administrators.

Appendix G: Monthly Summary of Financial Indicators

Monthly Summary of Financial Indicators

March 2009

	March Hours	YTD Hours	Value of YTD Hours	March Billings	YTD Billings	Billing Realization	March Receipts	YTD Receipts	Collection Realization	TYD Originations	Current WIP
Partner A	145	402	100,500	57,340	148,230	89%	42,356	189,459	89%	120,674	47,630
Partner B	123	375	84,375	38,900	127,870	74%	47,890	106,409	97%	209,200	34,583
Partner C	107	351	70,200	49,200	168,245	83%	52,560	167,980	92%	114,471	163,290
Associate D	184	548	95,900								
Associate E	137	429	75,075								
Paralegal F	127	394	39,400								
Paralegal G	135	419	41,900								
Firm Totals	958	2,918	507,350	145,440	444,345	80%	142,806	463,848	91%	444,345	245,503

Assumptions

Hourly Rates: Partner A $250; Partner B $225; Partner C $200; Associate $175; Paralegals $100
Partners get credit for and have responsibility for Associate and Paralegal time billed
Associates and Paralegals are evaluated on hours billed and quality of work; responsibility for write-offs remain with the billing Partner

Appendix H: Monthly Summary of Financial Data

Memorandum

To: Partners

From: Managing Partners

Date: April 9, 2009

Re: Monthly Financial Summary

I attach the March Monthly Summary of Financial Indicators, along with the normal monthly back-up reports, which provide additional detail.

Billable hours recorded for the first three months are running behind 2008 by approximately 12%. This is particularly alarming because the lawyers and paralegals took more vacation time in the first quarter of 2008 compared to the same three months in 2009. This may be an early warning that the firm's business may be off this year. A review of workloads and new cases will be on the agenda for our next partnership meeting.

Our billing realization is running about 5% lower than during the same period last year. The area of biggest concern continues to be our litigation practice. I cannot tell if this decline is the result of cases we should not have taken or whether too much of Associate E's time is being written off.

Taking a look at revenues to date, we are 7% behind budget and that shortfall is being offset by savings on the expense budget. Partner A expects a large fee in May, which may help, but the summer slump will soon be on us.

Based on the economy and what I have learned from other managing partners in the area, we are not alone in our struggles. Our goal, however, has to be to further analyze our financial position and be prepared to take some corrective actions before the problems become more serious. We have not been on our line of credit, but if the present trend continues we will be on the line by July, even with Partner A's expected large fee.

Appendix I: Compensation System Study Memo

Memorandum

To: Partners

From: Managing Partner

Date: May 23, 2009

Re: Partner Compensation System

You will recall that at this past year-end, several of you raised concerns about our partner compensation system. As a result of those discussions, we decided to establish a committee to study our current compensation system and be prepared to make recommendations at our Fall retreat. If changes are adopted, they will be effective for calendar year 2010.

The committee members, selected at our recent partnership meeting, are Partner D, Partner G, Partner J and me. We will review current literature, evaluate the recent results of our current system, solicit views from each of you at individual meetings, and consider making recommendations for change at the Annual Retreat. The committee has no preconceived opinion and is open to major change, minor tweaking, or no change at all. We do, however, understand that any change in the compensation system must be taken with caution and only with broad support from the vast majority of the partners.

There are several attachments to this memo. We have included two well-written articles on Partner Compensation methods. You will note that the articles do not espouse any particular method, but rather explore the options and describe the advantages and disadvantages of each.

We will be arranging individual meetings with each of you during the next 3 to 4 weeks. Please plan on meetings of $1^1/_2$ to 2 hours.

Appendix J:
Compensation Study
Committee Outline
of Questions

This outline of questions has been prepared for the compensation committee members to use in the confidential individual partner meetings. It represents a guide and a starting point, recognizing that it will be important to let the discussion develop and follow-up in ways that will insure each partner has an opportunity to express all of his or her opinions concerning partner compensation.

1. What behaviors of partners do we want to encourage and reward?
2. What partner behaviors do we want to discourage and penalize?
3. How well does our current compensation system encourage or discourage these behaviors?
4. What do you see as the advantages and disadvantages to a formula compensation system?
5. What do you see as the advantages and disadvantages to a subjective system?
6. Are you satisfied with the current system and how it operates? If, not, what problems can you identify?
7. To the extent you know, how satisfied are the other partners with the compensation system and how it operates? If other partners are not satisfied, what problem(s) can you identify?
8. What specific changes in the compensation system or its operation would you like the committee to consider?
9. Are there any other matters or considerations you would like to bring to the attention of the committee?

Appendix K:
Table of Contents
for Compensation
Study Report

Appendix L: Compensation Study Committee Retreat Agenda

1. Introduction
2. Report on Study Committee Activity
   a. Research
   b. Partner Interviews
   c. Discussion of Compensation Plan Goals
      i. Desired Behaviors to be Rewarded
      ii. Unwanted Behaviors to be Penalized
3. Recommendations of Study Committee
   a. Describe Proposed Compensation System
      i. System for Allocation of Profits
      ii. The Process for Allocating Profits
   b. Discussion of Proposed Compensation System
4. Vote
5. Implementation Plan

Appendix M: Formula Compensation System

The Partner compensation system is based on a formula designed to track the revenue contributions of the individual Partners. During the course of the year, each Partner will receive a draw, as determined by the Management Committee, which will be based on historical performance and intended to equal approximately 70% of each Partner's projected compensation for the given year. The individual Partner's account will be reconciled at year end, based on the following formula:

1. Each Partner's total annual compensation shall be determined retroactively at the close of each year.
2. In the year end reconciliation, each Partner will get credit for the payment of fees (not including expenses) received during the year as follows:
   a. A Working Partner Credit of 80% of the payment of fees for the work performed, including payments for the work of associates and/or paralegals managed by that Partner.
   b. An Origination Credit of 20% of the total payment of fees to the Partner originating the client.
   c. Once the total credits have been calculated, they will be converted to percentages that total 100%.
3. The Management Committee shall examine revenue and expenses and determine the amount of total compensation available for distribution to the Partners.
4. The Management Committee shall then apply each Partner's percentage to the total amount of compensation available for distribution.
   a. Partners whose draw for the year exceeds their percentage share of the total compensation available for distribution shall pay back to the Firm the amount of the excess.

    b. Partners whose draw for the year has been less than their percentage share of the total compensation available for distribution shall receive the balance.

5. (OPTIONAL) The Partners recognize that the formula set out in Paragraph 4 does not reward those Partners who serve in the important function of managing the Firm. In order to reward those efforts, the Partners have at the beginning of each year set a dollar amount to be added to the formula share to be received by the Managing Partner and (if applicable) each Management Committee Member. Prior to calculating the amount of compensation available for distribution under the formula, an amount equal to the additional payments to the Managing Partner and/or the Management Committee Members shall be subtracted and treated as an expense for purpose of determining the amounts distributed under the formula.

Appendix N: Subjective Compensation System

The Firm has adopted a subjective compensation system for rewarding Partners for their contribution to the Firm's success. It is important that the factors affecting the allocation of income and the process of implementation are clearly understood by all lawyers, including new lawyers who have joined the firm since the last discussion.

Compensation Factors

The most significant factors to be considered in allocating compensation are described in three categories. They are not ranked in terms of importance.

Productivity

Productivity can be based on objective data concerning meeting billable hour goals, meeting cash receipts goals, attaining profitability goals, and originating clients for the firm. Productivity also includes effective delegation of work to other lawyers and paralegals, which will increase our efficiency and lead to the development of the newer members of the firm. The assessment of productivity must also recognize the <u>results</u> of successful marketing and client retention efforts.

Quality of Professional Effort

Quality of Professional Effort category includes a broad encompassing notion of professional competence in one's practice and good practice management. The term includes high ethical standards, dedicated and effective service to firm clients and good judgment in dealing with and solving client problems. This category includes attending to all of the day-to-day tasks, carefully managing one's time, effectively organizing and managing projects, tending to accurate time-keeping and billing, and complying with all firm administrative policies and priorities.

Leadership

Firm Leadership is the demonstrated effectiveness in promoting the objectives of the firm as a whole. Effective leadership may come from those members of the firm who can in their own distinctive ways contribute significantly to the consensus and direction of the firm efforts. Leadership can be by highly visible service in administration positions, or quiet effective leadership by example.

Process

The determination of the allocation of income among the Firm's partners is the responsibility of the Partners. In order to facilitate the process, the Partners delegate to the Management Committee the responsibility of conducting evaluations, assisting in the development of lawyer annual plans and making income allocation recommendations to the Partners. The following process will take place in January of each year:

- The Management Committee will distribute to each Partner a Profile Form and an Annual Plan Worksheet to be completed and returned to the Committee within 10 days. The Forms are designed to elicit relevant information from the Partner that should be considered in the income allocation process and in the development of the Partner's plan for the coming year.
- One member of the Management Committee will meet with each Partner to discuss the Profile Form and the Annual Plan Worksheet and to receive any additional input the Partner has concerning his or her own contribution to the firm or the contribution of any other Partner in the firm.
- The Management Committee will meet to review the income allocation factors and decide upon its recommendations to the full partnership concerning (i) each lawyer's evaluation, (ii) any adjustments to their income, and (iii) suggestions with regard to the content of each Partner's annual plan for the following year. Members of the Committee will report the results of their interviews. The firm's administrator will attend the meeting to provide information and data as requested by Committee members. Each evaluation will be reduced to a written paragraph to be delivered to the Partner. The tone of the written evaluations should be constructive in nature.
- One member of the Management Committee will meet with each Partner (i) to deliver and discuss the results of the evaluation, (ii) to describe any adjustment in the Partner's compensation and (iii) to work with the Partner to complete the Annual Plan, consistent with the needs of the firm as identified by the Management Committee. The Annual Plan will be reduced to writing and agreed to by the Partner and the Management Committee. The Annual Plan will be utilized as a consideration in the Partner's evaluation the following year.
- Following the individual Partner meetings, the Management Committee will present its recommendations for adjustments to Partner compensation to the partnership at a meeting held no later than the first week of February. Following the vote of the Partnership, any changes to compensation will be applied retroactively to January 1 of that year.

Appendix O:
Partner Profile Form

TO: Management Committee

FROM: _____

DATE: _____

1. Describe your professional efforts during 200_ to advance the goals of the Firm, making reference to both your personal productivity, as well as other contributions to the success of the firm as a whole.

2. Briefly set forth any other matters that you feel should bear on your compensation for next year.

3. Describe what additional contributions you can make to the success of the firm which the Management Committee should have in mind as it works with you to create your Annual Plan for 200_.

Appendix P: Partner Evaluation

CONFIDENTIAL

Partner X has improved his/her productivity over prior years. He/she has demonstrated a solid commitment to the hourly goals set by the firm, which has had a direct result on his/her revenue production. However, a noticeable increase in accounts receivable appears to reflect a need for improvement in screening clients on in-take. This may be symptomatic of his/her practice area but needs attention.

Family law is a difficult area, but the firm is supportive of promoting his/her practice with a plan to develop clients who are better able to afford his/her services. In the effort to move the practice to a higher level, Partner X is encouraged to decline representation of clients that cannot afford his/her services. There are a number of competent family law practitioners who have lower overhead and can serve that market. An increase in the standard fee deposit may help eliminate the clients who later become receivable problems.

He/she has been an example for others in her effective mentoring of Associate Y, who had been struggling prior to this past year. On a firm-wide basis, he/she has made a significant contribution by taking on responsibility for organizing the summer intern program, which has resulted in nothing but positive feedback.

Appendix Q: Partner Annual Plan Worksheet

CONFIDENTIAL

Lawyer _____   Year _____

Outline the skills, expertise, and concentration of your practice, making note of any anticipated changes:

Describe your expectations for serving clients in your field of practice next year:

What efforts do you expect to undertake next year to:
- Enhance your skills
- Expand your practice
- Improve your productivity
- Assist others in improving their practices
- Assume responsibilities within the firm
- Advance the goals of the firm
- Participate in civic and professional matters

Please provide information about your anticipated productivity that the Management Committee can consider in developing the Firm's revenue budget:

Billable Hours _____   Originations $_____
Client Files Managed $_____   Realization Rate ____%

Appendix R:
Annual Partner Plan

Partner _____   Year _____

Expectations with regard to service of clients:

Agreed plan to:

- Enhance your skills
- Expand your practice
- Improve your productivity
- Assist others in improving their practices
- Assume responsibilities within the firm
- Advance the goals of the firm
- Participate in civic and professional matters

Productivity expectations:

Billable Hours _____   Originations $_____
Client Files Managed $_____   Realization Rate _____%

Accepted by Partner: _____
Approved by Management Committee: _____
Dated: January _____, 200_

Appendix S: Associate Orientation Program

The orientation of all new lawyers shall be mandatory and is designed for the purpose of demonstrating to the hire a unified and organized welcome, which provides everything that is needed to begin work. It is desirable to develop an orientation manual containing information that will cover or supplement the required topics. Orientation may be offered in full day or part day sessions.

1. Complete tour of facilities and introductions to firm members
2. Meet with the office manager or legal administrator to review the following:
   - Salary/Benefits
   - Work schedule/holidays/social functions
   - Firm history/structure/identify key individuals
   - Secretaries, paralegals and other support
   - Telephone, computer, and other office systems
   - Firm filing systems
   - Library and information management
   - The docket system
   - Other matters of importance
3. Meet with lawyer(s) concerning the following:
   - Time recording
   - General billing procedures
   - Confidentiality
   - Office meetings
   - Training programs
   - Firm's social events
   - Work assignments
   - Mentoring program
   - Memberships/dues/CLE's
   - Pro bono
   - Evaluation process/bonuses

4. Meet with Department Heads or Heads of Practice Groups to address the following:
   - Specifics as to Billing: How to charge time, expenses, disbursements, write-offs, descriptions of work
   - Workings of the departments or group, including meetings, policies and procedures
5. Meet with other staff members to address particular policies and procedures. For example, in larger firms, Librarian, Human Resources Director, IT Department member, Paralegal Manager, Docket Control Clerk, etc.

Appendix T: Associate Mentoring Program

The firm is committed to an Associate Mentoring program. As part of the associate's career development and training, the Firm has adopted a policy providing each first year associate a Mentor/Mentee opportunity aimed at the following goals:

- Develop skills and knowledge that will assist him/her to become a successful lawyer with the firm
- Develop the skills necessary to become a leader in the firm
- Develop an understanding of the culture of the firm
- Develop a full understanding of all firm policies and procedures
- Learn the firm's philosophy regarding client service and how it is achieved

The Roles of the Mentor and Mentee are provided below. Specific responsibilities are fully outlined in the Program Manual.

The Role of the Mentor:

- Help the mentee to understand the firm's expectations of associates.
- Help the mentee integrate into the firm.
- Guide the associate mentee through his or her development as a lawyer, including gaining the skills and knowledge to become an ethical and qualified lawyer.
- Assist the associate to develop a career path and build a practice by providing guidance in developing the tools to do both.
- Help associates to gain the confidence and experience to become a leader in the firm.
- Act as a positive role model.

The Role of the Mentee:

- Be willing to learn from the mentor.
- Be willing to ask questions of the mentor.
- Discuss personal and professional goals.
- Be committed to personal and career growth, as well as the overall success of the firm.
- Be willing to accept direction and constructive feedback.
- Be proactive.

Note: I would like to thank my partner Sandra J. Boyer from Boyer Greene L.L.C. for providing this Sample Associate Mentoring Program, which relates to consulting work she performs assisting firms in recruiting, transitioning, and counseling legal administrators.

Appendix U:
Associate Task
Performance List

A litigation associate must be capable of accomplishing tasks specific to a litigation case. These tasks include preparation of various documents, including the following:

Simple complaint
Multiparty pleading
Answer to a complaint
Set of interrogatories
Answers to interrogatories
Motion to dismiss
Motion raising jurisdictional issues
Request for production of documents
Trial brief
Appellate brief
Appeal to an appellate court
Trial notebook
Memorandum outlining settlement strategy
Plan for an interview with a client
Status letter to client
Case Plan
Mediation Statement
Various Motions, including a Motion to Compel Discovery
Response to a request for production
Request for admissions
Answer to a request for admissions

Additional tasks include the following:

Conduct a client interview
Conduct and defend a deposition
Prepare witnesses for testimony at trial
Attend a pre-trial hearing

Argue a document production controversy
Attend an administrative hearing
Try a small claims court case
Try an arbitration case
Participate in a mediation conference
Second chair a trial
Participate in a trial alone
Attend a settlement negotiation
Try a personal injury case
Participate in an equity hearing
Participate in a federal court proceeding
Argue a motion for a new trial or judgment n.o.v.
Participate in a bankruptcy proceeding
Handle *a pro bono matter*
Represent an indigent defendant in a criminal court with appropriate supervision
Prepare a memorandum on a litigation ethical problem
Participate in a litigation CLE seminar

Appendix V:
Associate Training Policy

The firm is committed to an Associate Training program focused on training and career development. As part of the program, the Firm has adopted a policy allowing each first and second year associate training hours, separate and apart from those hours billed to a client.

Each Associate, in their first two years of practice, will have an annual billable hour requirement of 1,800 hours, made up of 1,500 billable hours and 300 training hours. The Practice Groups will have responsibility for the implementation of the program, as follows:

1. Each Practice Group Chair will work with each of the associates assigned to the Group to insure that each Associate is exposed to the types of work necessary to a successful practice.
2. As part of the program, the Practice Group Chair will have the authority and the responsibility to approve assignments for each Associate, of up to 300 hours per year, which will be designated training hours and will not be billed to the client.
3. Partners within each Practice Group may request that an Associate be assigned to a file on a training basis by preparing and submitting the proper application to the Chair.
4. In the alternative, the Chair may initiate the process by requesting that a Partner work with an associate on a training basis when, in the opinion of the Chair, the exposure to the work will be valuable to the associate.

The goal of the program is to provide valuable experiences to Associates in circumstances where billable hours from the Associate cannot be justified to the client. In approving the training assignments, it will be the responsibility of the Chair of each Practice Group to make sure that the reason for the assignment is the value to the associate and not the needs of the Partner.

Appendix W:
Associate Evaluation Form

CONFIDENTIAL

Name of Associate _____

Name of Evaluator _____

Date _____

Level of Working Contact in Last 12 months: None ____
Limited ____
Moderate ____
Extensive ____

	Excellent	V. Good	Good	Fair	Poor	N/A
Dedication to Client Service and Goals of Firm						
Knowledge and Application of Legal Principles						
Writing Skills/Organization/ Accuracy/Style						
Verbal Skills/Persuasion/ Client Impression						
Reliability/Timeliness/Efficiency						
Ability to Handle Assignment/ Contact with Partners						
Initiative/Judgment/ Common Sense						
Attitude toward Partners, Associates and Staff						
Mastery of Office Systems and Office Technology						
Involvement in Professional and Community Activities						
Potential for Partnership (for 3+ yr associates)						

Specific Comments _____

_____

_____

_____

_____

_____

_____

_____

_____

_____

_____

_____

_____

Note: I would like to thank my partner Sandra J. Boyer from Boyer Greene L.L.C. for providing this Associate Evaluation Form, which relates to consulting work she performs assisting firms in recruiting, transitioning, and counseling legal administrators.

Appendix X:
Criteria for Partnership

Partnership in the law firm of _____
signifies that person has both qualified to become and has accepted the responsibilities of an owner of the firm. Every Associate hired by the firm has an opportunity to become a Partner, if and when the Associate meets all of the following criteria:

1. Has practiced law for a minimum of five (5) years,
2. Has practiced law with _____
   for at least two (2) years,
3. Has demonstrated a high level of competence and skill in the designated practice area,
4. Provides quality client service and has the ability to nurture and expand client relationships,
5. Demonstrates an ability to develop a self sustaining practice,
6. Commits to marketing the firm (not just self) and shows the potential of producing business for other lawyers in the firm,
7. Acts in a collaborative, team-oriented manner, complying with firm policies, systems and procedures, treating all lawyers and staff with respect,
8. Commits to the training and supervision of others,
9. Demonstrates a high level of commitment to management and shows potential for making a positive contribution in some aspect of the firm's management,
10. Puts the firm's interests first, ahead of one's individual interests, and
11. Satisfies a need within the firm.

Appendix Y:
Practice Group Agenda

1. Review of New Cases
2. Discuss Work Loads
   a. Associates
   b. Paralegals
3. Report on Recent Supreme Court Decisions
4. Report on CLE's Attended
5. Discuss Practice Group Projects
   a. Discuss Marketing Initiatives
   b. Review Need for Upgraded Computer Software
6. Other Matters

Appendix Z:
Practice Group Agenda—
Extended Topics

1. Review of New Cases
2. Discuss Financial Performance of Practice Group
   a. Review of Practice Group Financial Reports, including Billings, Revenues, Realization, Write-offs, Work-in-Process, Hours Recorded
   b. Discuss Work Loads: Partners, Associates, Paralegals
   c. Discuss Available Resources
      i. Consider Request to Management Committee for Additional Paralegal
      ii. Discuss Need for Additional Library Resources
3. Report on Recent Supreme Court Decisions
4. Report on CLE's Attended
5. Discuss Practice Group Projects
   a. Discuss Marketing Initiatives
   b. Review Need for Upgraded Computer Software
   c. Discuss Billing Rate Study
6. Other Matters

Index

The Lawyer's Guide to Increasing Revenue: Unlocking the Profit Potential in Your Firm

By Arthur G. Greene

If you are ready to look beyond cost-cutting and short-term solutions, and toward new revenue opportunities, then *The Lawyer's Guide to Increasing Revenue* will show you how you can achieve growth using the resources you already have at your firm. Discover the factors that affect your law firm's revenue production, how to evaluate them, and how to take specific action steps designed to increase your returns. The book will also show you how to fully develop your plans into a multi-year strategy for improved long-term financial results.

Paralegals, Profitability, and the Future of Your Law Practice

By Arthur G. Greene and Therese A. Cannon

Effectively integrate paralegals into your practice, and expand their roles to ensure your firm is successful in the next decade with this essential resource. If you're not currently using paralegals, you'll learn why you need them and how to create and implement a successful paralegal model in your practice. If you're already using paralegals, you'll learn how to ensure your paralegal program is structured properly, runs effectively, and continually contributes to your bottom line. Valuable appendices contain sample job descriptions, model guidelines, confidentiality agreements, performance evaluations, and other useful resources, also provided on the accompanying CD-ROM for ease in implementation!

Results-Oriented Financial Management: A Step-By-Step Guide to Law Firm Profitability, Second Edition

By John G. Iezzi, CPA

This hands-on, how-to book will assist managing partners, law firm managers, and law firm accountants by providing them with the budgeting and financial knowledge they need to need to make the critical decisions. Whether you're a financial novice or veteran manager, this book will help you examine every facet of your financial affairs from cash flow and budget creation to billing and compensation. Also included with the book are valuable financial models on CD-ROM allowing you to compute profitability and determine budgets by inputting your own data. The appendix contains useful forms and examples from lawyers who have actually implemented alternative billing methods at their firms.

Collecting Your Fee: Getting Paid From Intake to Invoice.

By Edward Poll

This practical and user-friendly guide provides you with proven strategies and sound advice that will make the process of collecting your fees simpler, easier, and more effective! This handy resource provides you with the framework around which to structure your collection efforts. You'll learn how you can streamline your billing and collection process by hiring the appropriate staff, establishing strong client relationships from the start, and issuing client-friendly invoices. In addition, you'll benefit from the strategies to use when the client fails to pay the bill on time and what you need to do to get paid when all else fails. Also included is a CD-ROM with sample forms, letters, agreements, and more for you to customize to your own practice needs.

Compensation Plans for Law Firms, Fourth Edition

By James D. Cotterman, Altman Weil, Inc.

This newly updated fourth edition of *Compensation Plans for Law Firms* examines the continually evolving compensation landscape and the concepts that will affect your law firm most. You'll take an extensive look at the world of law firm compensation, including:

- Compensation theory
- The art and science of compensation
- Partner and shareholder compensation
- Of Counsel compensation
- Associate compensation
- Paralegal compensation
- Staff compensation
- Bonuses, increases, and incentives
- Debt, taxes, retirement, and withdrawal
- Evaluations, fairness and flexibility
- . . . and much more!

Risk Management: Survival Tools for Law Firms, Second Edition

By Anthony E. Davis and Peter R. Jarvis

This book helps your firm establish solid policies, procedures, and systems to minimize risk. This completely revised edition and accompanying CD provides a comprehensive overview of risk management, offers a practical approach to risk management evaluation, and steps to take to create a "best practice" plan. Using a practical self-audit tool, the book enables lawyers to consider how well their firms are addressing each of the key components of effective risk management.

The Essential Formbook:
Comprehensive Management Tools for Lawyers
Volume I: Partnership and Organizational
Agreements/Client Intake and Fee Agreements
Volume II: Human Resources/
Fees, Billing, and Collection
Volume III: Calendar and File Management/
Law Firm Financial Analysis
Volume IV: Disaster Planning and Recovery/
Risk Management and Professional Liability Insurance
By Gary A. Munneke and Anthony E. Davis
Useful to legal practitioners of all specialties and sizes, these volumes will help you establish profitable, affirmative client relationships so you can avoid unnecessary risks associated with malpractice and disciplinary complaints. And, with all the forms available on CD-ROM, it's easy to modify them to match your specific needs. Visit our Web site at www.lawpractice.org/catalog/511-0424 for more information about this invaluable resource.

The Lawyer's Guide to Strategic Planning:
Defining, Setting, and Achieving Your Firm's Goals
By Thomas C. Grella and Michael L. Hudkins
This practice-building resource is your guide to planning dynamic strategic plans and implementing them at your firm. You'll learn about the actual planning process and how to establish goals in key planning areas such as law firm governance, competition, opening a new office, financial management, technology, marketing and competitive intelligence, client development and retention, and more. The accompanying CD-ROM contains a wealth of policies, statements, and other sample documents. If you're serious about improving the way your firm works, increasing productivity, making better decisions, and setting your firm on the right course—this is the resource you need.

Managing Partner 101: A Guide to Successful Law Firm Leadership, Second Edition
By Lawrence G. Green
Typically, lawyer managers in a firm have few, if any, opportunities for formal management training. The leaders in a law firm all too often lack the education in finance, ethics, and leadership they need to run a business. *Managing Partner 101: A Leadership Guide for Building the Successful Law Firm*, offers suggestions, tips, and the basic ground rules for any lawyers who must manage other lawyers.

Winning Alternatives to the Billable Hour:
Strategies that Work, Third Edition
By Mark A. Robertson and James A. Calloway
Your entire practice is based on doing battle for your clients. Unfortunately, the issues that arise when it comes to assessing the value of these protective and beneficial services are a source of contention for both yourself and your clients. This newly revised third edition of the highly acclaimed *Winning Alternatives to the Billable Hour: Strategies that Work*, provides you with tools you can use in your practice to implement and evaluate alternative billing methods, including real case studies of lawyers and firms successfully using alternative billing to deliver value to both the client and the lawyer.

The ABA Guide to Lawyer Trust Accounts
By Jay G Foonberg
Avoid the pitfalls of trust account rules violations! Designed as a self-study course or as seminar materials, with short, stand-alone chapters that walk you through the procedures of client trust accounting. This indispensable reference outlines the history of applicable ethics rules; how you could inadvertently be violating those rules; ways to work with your banker and accountant to set up the office systems you need; numerous forms that you can adapt for your office (including self-tests for seminars and CLE credits); plus Foonberg's "10 rules of good trust account procedures" and "10 steps to good trust account records"—intended to work with whatever local rules your state mandates.

The Lawyer's Guide to Marketing Your Practice,
Second Edition
Edited by James A. Durham and Deborah McMurray
This book is packed with practical ideas, innovative strategies, useful checklists, and sample marketing and action plans to help you implement a successful, multi-faceted, and profit-enhancing marketing plan for your firm. Organized into four sections, this illuminating resource covers: Developing Your Approach; Enhancing Your Image; Implementing Marketing Strategies and Maintaining Your Program. Appendix materials include an instructive primer on market research to inform you on research methodologies that support the marketing of legal services. The accompanying CD-ROM contains a wealth of checklists, plans, and other sample reports, questionnaires, and templates—all designed to make implementing your marketing strategy as easy as possible.

30-Day Risk-Free Order Form
Call Today! 1-800-285-2221
Monday–Friday, 7:30 AM – 5:30 PM, Central Time

Qty	Title	LPM Price	Regular Price	Total
_____	ABA Guide to Lawyer Trust Accounts (5110374)	$ 69.95	$ 79.95	$_____
_____	Managing Partner 101: A Guide to Successful Law Firm Leadership, Second Edition (5110451)	44.95	49.95	$_____
_____	Collecting Your Fee: Getting Paid From Intake to Invoice (5110490)	69.95	79.95	$_____
_____	The Essential Formbook, Volume I (5110424V1)	169.95	199.95	$_____
_____	The Essential Formbook, Volume II (5110424V2)	169.95	199.95	$_____
_____	The Essential Formbook, Volume III (5110424V3)	169.95	199.95	$_____
_____	The Essential Formbook, Volume IV (5110424V4)	169.95	199.95	$_____
_____	The Lawyer's Guide to Increasing Revenue: Unlocking the Profit Potential in Your Firm (5110521)	59.95	79.95	$_____
_____	Compensation Plans for Law Firms, Fourth Edition (5110507)	79.95	94.95	$_____
_____	The Lawyer's Guide to Marketing Your Practice, Second Edition (5110500)	79.95	89.95	$_____
_____	The Lawyer's Guide to Strategic Planning (5110520)	59.95	79.95	$_____
_____	Paralegals, Profitability, and the Future of Your Law Practice (5110491)	59.95	69.95	$_____
_____	Results-Oriented Financial Management, Second Edition (5110493)	89.95	99.95	$_____
_____	Winning Alternatives to the Billable Hour: Strategies that Work, Third Edition (5110660)	74.95	99.95	$_____
_____	Risk Management: Survival Tools for Law Firms, Second Edition (5110653)	79.95	89.95	$_____

*Postage and Handling	
$10.00 to $24.99	$5.95
$25.00 to $49.99	$9.95
$50.00 to $99.99	$12.95
$100.00 to $349.99	$17.95
$350 to $499.99	$24.95

**Tax
DC residents add 5.75%
IL residents add 9.00%

*Postage and Handling	$_____
**Tax	$_____
TOTAL	$_____

PAYMENT

❏ Check enclosed (to the ABA)

❏ Visa ❏ MasterCard ❏ American Express

_____
Account Number   Exp. Date   Signature

Name _____ Firm _____
Address _____
City _____ State _____ Zip _____
Phone Number _____ E-Mail Address _____

Note: E-Mail address is required if ordering the
The Lawyer's Guide to Fact Finding on the Internet
E-mail Newsletter (5110498)

Guarantee
If—for any reason—you are not satisfied with your purchase, you may return it within 30 days of receipt for a complete refund of the price of the book(s). No questions asked!

Mail: ABA Publication Orders, P.O. Box 10892, Chicago, Illinois 60610-0892
♦ Phone: 1-800-285-2221 ♦ FAX: 312-988-5568

E-Mail: abasvcctr@abanet.org ♦ Internet: http://www.lawpractice.org/catalog

Are You in Your Element?

Tap into the Resources of the ABA Law Practice Management Section

ABA Law Practice Management Section Membership Benefits

The ABA Law Practice Management Section (LPM) is a professional membership organization of the American Bar Association that helps lawyers and other legal professionals with the business of practicing law. LPM focuses on providing information and resources in the core areas of marketing, management, technology, and finance through its award-winning magazine, teleconference series, Webzine, educational programs (CLE), Web site, and publishing division. For more than thirty years, LPM has established itself as a leader within the ABA and the profession-at-large by producing the world's largest legal technology conference (ABA TECHSHOW®) each year. In addition, LPM's publishing program is one of the largest in the ABA, with more than eighty-five titles in print.

In addition to significant book discounts, LPM Section membership offers these benefits:

ABA TECHSHOW
Membership includes a $100 discount to ABA TECHSHOW, the world's largest legal technology conference & expo!

Teleconference Series
Convenient, monthly CLE teleconferences on hot topics in marketing, management, technology and finance. Access educational opportunities from the comfort of your office chair – today's practical way to earn CLE credits!

LAW|PRACTICE
THE BUSINESS OF PRACTICING LAW

Law Practice Magazine
Eight issues of our award-winning *Law Practice* magazine, full of insightful articles and practical tips on Marketing/Client Development, Practice Management, Legal Technology, and Finance.

Law Practice TODAY

Law Practice Today
LPM's unique Web-based magazine covers all the hot topics in law practice management today — identify current issues, face today's challenges, find solutions quickly. Visit www.lawpracticetoday.org.

LAW TECHNOLOGY TODAY
EDD, LITIGATION SUPPORT AND LAW OFFICE TECHNOLOGY

Law Technology Today
LPM's newest Webzine focuses on legal technology issues in law practice management — covering a broad spectrum of the technology, tools, strategies and their implementation to help lawyers build a successful practice. Visit www.lawtechnologytoday.org.

LawPractice.news
Monthly news and information from the ABA Law Practice Management Section

LawPractice.news
Brings Section news, educational opportunities, book releases, and special offers to members via e-mail each month.

To learn more about the ABA Law Practice Management Section, visit www.lawpractice.org or call 1-800-285-2221.

MARKETING • MANAGEMENT • TECHNOLOGY • FINANCE

ABA LAW PRACTICE MANAGEMENT SECTION
MARKETING • MANAGEMENT • TECHNOLOGY • FINANCE

About the CD

The accompanying CD contains the text of the Appendices from *The Lawyer's Guide to Governing Your Firm*. The files are in Microsoft Word® format.

For additional information about the files on the CD, please open and read the "**readme.doc**" file on the CD.

NOTE: The set of files on the CD may only be used on a single computer or moved to and used on another computer. Under no circumstances may the set of files be used on more than one computer at one time. If you are interested in obtaining a license to use the set of files on a local network, please contact: Director, Copyrights and Contracts, American Bar Association, 321 N. Clark Street, Chicago, IL 60654, (312) 988-6101. **Please read the license and warranty statements on the following page before using this CD.**

**Defending Liberty
Pursuing Justice**

CD-ROM to accompany
The Lawyer's Guide to Governing Your Firm

WARNING: Opening this package indicates your understanding and acceptance of the following Terms and Conditions.

READ THE FOLLOWING TERMS AND CONDITIONS BEFORE OPENING THIS SEALED PACKAGE. IF YOU DO NOT AGREE WITH THEM, PROMPTLY RETURN THE UNOPENED PACKAGE TO EITHER THE PARTY FROM WHOM IT WAS ACQUIRED OR TO THE AMERICAN BAR ASSOCIATION AND YOUR MONEY WILL BE RETURNED.

The document files in this package are a proprietary product of the American Bar Association and are protected by Copyright Law. The American Bar Association retains title to and ownership of these files.

License

You may use this set of files on a single computer or move it to and use it on another computer, but under no circumstances may you use the set of files on more than one computer at the same time. You may copy the files either in support of your use of the files on a single computer or for backup purposes. If you are interested in obtaining a license to use the set of files on a local network, please contact: Manager, Publication Policies & Contracting, American Bar Association, 321 N. Clark Street, Chicago, IL 60654, (312) 988-6101.

You may permanently transfer the set of files to another party if the other party agrees to accept the terms and conditions of this License Agreement. If you transfer the set of files, you must at the same time transfer all copies of the files to the same party or destroy those not transferred. Such transfer terminates your license. You may not rent, lease, assign or otherwise transfer the files except as stated in this paragraph.

You may modify these files for your own use within the provisions of this License Agreement. You may not redistribute any modified files.

Warranty

If a CD-ROM in this package is defective, the American Bar Association will replace it at no charge if the defective diskette is returned to the American Bar Association within 60 days from the date of acquisition.

American Bar Association warrants that these files will perform in substantial compliance with the documentation supplied in this package. However, the American Bar Association does not warrant these forms as to the correctness of the legal material contained therein. If you report a significant defect in performance in writing to the American Bar Association, and the American Bar Association is not able to correct it within 60 days, you may return the CD, including all copies and documentation, to the American Bar Association and the American Bar Association will refund your money.

Any files that you modify will no longer be covered under this warranty even if they were modified in accordance with the License Agreement and product documentation.

IN NO EVENT WILL THE AMERICAN BAR ASSOCIATION, ITS OFFICERS, MEMBERS, OR EMPLOYEES BE LIABLE TO YOU FOR ANY DAMAGES, INCLUDING LOST PROFITS, LOST SAVINGS OR OTHER IN-CIDENTAL OR CONSEQUENTIAL DAMAGES ARISING OUT OF YOUR USE OR INABILITY TO USE THESE FILES EVEN IF THE AMERICAN BAR ASSOCIATION OR AN AUTHORIZED AMERICAN BAR AS-SOCIATION REPRESENTATIVE HAS BEEN ADVISED OF THE POSSIBILITY OF SUCH DAMAGES, OR FOR ANY CLAIM BY ANY OTHER PARTY. SOME STATES DO NOT ALLOW THE LIMITATION OR EX-CLUSION OF LIABILITY FOR INCIDENTAL OR CONSEQUENTIAL DAMAGES, IN WHICH CASE THIS LIMITATION MAY NOT APPLY TO YOU.